Glass Candlesticks

of the
DEPRESSION ERA

IDENTIFICATION AND VALUE GUIDE

GENE FLORENCE

COLLECTOR BOOKS

A Division of Schroeder Publishing Co., Inc.

The current values in this book should be used only as a guide. They are not intended to set prices, which vary from one section of the country to another. Auction prices as well as dealer prices vary greatly and are affected by condition and demand. Neither the author nor the publisher assumes responsibility for any losses which might be incurred as a result of consulting this guide.

Searching For A Publisher?

We are always looking for knowledgeable people considered experts within their fields. If you feel that there is a real need for a book on your collectible subject and have a large comprehensive collection, contact Collector Books.

Cover Design: Beth Summers

Collector Books
P.O. Box 3009
Paducah, KY 42002-3009

Copyright © 2000 by Gene Florence

Contents

Preface

The idea for a candlestick book has been on the back burner for several years. Collectors have asked me when I was going to do a book on candlesticks, and I have told them "some day." Well, that day has finally arrived, with the personal help of several friends who have loaned me candlesticks from their collections. This book is barely a beginning in the vast world of American glass candlesticks. There will be additional volumes if this book is accepted (meaning bought) by collectors and/or dealers. So we'll see how eager the collecting world is for such a reference.

This book covers all forms of candles, from candlesticks to candelabra. Terminology used in this book is always that of the company catalogs if possible and not necessarily the terms that the present world acknowledges. I was taught Latin where the ending -brum was singular and -bra was plural. This is not necessarily true in company catalogs; so please realize that I do know the difference even though it is confused herein at times.

You will find I have omitted many of the candles that have been pictured regularly in my other books. I will try to include them in later books, but I thought you would like to see more of the candles that are out there which are not in my books. Let me know how you like this! Your responses will go a long way in determining the direction of any future books.

How to Use This Book

This book is arranged by color, similar to the format of my stemware book. A few minor differences are incorporated such as all crystal is in one section whether decorated, satinized, cut, or etched. Within the color sections, candles are arranged by company and pattern. There are a few liberties taken within an individual company section in order to fit the category; but, all in all, this seems to be the easiest way for new (as well as seasoned) collectors to find an unknown candle for which they are searching. For example, if you have a blue candle (any shade of blue) go to that color section and look there first. If not there, try the crystal section next. There are more crystal candles pictured than any other types since there are more of those found.

If the candle has a name (true or nickname), we have generally used that first rather than the assigned company catalog number, though the catalog number (for both the candle blank and etching) is listed where known. You may also note that like numbered candle lines may have varying prices due to certain etches and/or colors being more desirable to collectors. All prices are for one candle and not a pair. Realize that colored candles are generally worth more than crystal, and that these prices are only a guide. Blue or red candles are usually more highly prized than amber, pink, or green. There are too many variables to price every color within the guidelines of this book. I had several dealers' opinions involved in helping price this book, but the final responsibility for any errors of omission or commission lies entirely with me.

Courtesy of information supplied by Barbara Adt Namon, notations have been included for a couple of known designers (George Sakier and Joseph Balda) whose work is beginning to exhibit added impact with knowledgeable collectors.

I hope you find this book a welcome addition to your reference library on glassware.

Acknowledgments

I have greatly benefited from the efforts of many people helping me assemble glass and data for my books. Cathy, my wife, has always been involved in sorting, packing, and unpacking glass both at home and at the photography sessions, plus editing each of my seventy books; and although she no longer has to type them, she makes sure they are easily understood by anyone whether they have knowledge about the glass or not. Were it not for her help, I would still be in the process of identifying candlesticks instead of finishing this book. No words can thank her enough for the drudge work she does anonymously! She pitched in and spent many hours researching line numbers and obscure pattern names for candlesticks while I was working on the fourteenth edition of my *Collector's Encyclopedia of Depression Glass* and the fifth edition of *Collectible Glassware from the 40s, 50s, and 60s*. These newer editions always take longer and longer to write in order to try to keep them interesting for new collectors as well as for those readers who have been following my books for years. Convincing anyone, other than someone who has rewritten a book, that this is true, is more difficult than doing it. Believe it or not, writing a book on a totally new topic is easier!

Most of the photographs herein were taken by Charley Lynch who is the official photographer for Collector Books. He generally likes to take individual pictures, but he gets hyper when he sees all the dangling prisms on some of the larger candlesticks. It takes a while for all of them to settle down every time the candle is positioned in a different way. It took months to get all these photos done. Thanks, Charley! Additionally, Neil Unger supplied some photos of candlesticks from his and Eddie's collection.

Many dealers have furnished candlesticks and pricing information for this book. I would particularly like to thank Dick and Pat Spencer, Dan Tucker and Lorrie Kitchen, Neil and Eddie Unger, Lynn Welker, Joe and Florence Solito, Kelly O'Kane, Kevin Kiley, Art and Shirley Moore, Ron Holmes, and Dan DePlanche. Dick Spencer wrapped and escorted candlesticks from Illinois to Paducah not once, but several times in the last year. Without the help of Dick and Pat, Heisey glassware would not be as well represented in my books.

The staff at Collector Books has worked tirelessly on this book. Della Wyatt helped set up a data base entry file so I could have a way to communicate to the staff (as well as you) on each of the 400+ candlesticks pictured herein. Beth Summers did the cover design. There were many shapes and sizes to deal with by the staff, as you can see by the variety of candles shown.

As with the stemware book, there were quantities of individual transparencies to sort and arrange. After all pictures were hand delivered, only six eventually turned up missing. I worked out that problem without a stroke. All additional quandaries were given to Collector Books editor Lisa Stroup. If I've overlooked anyone, forgive me. It was not intentional. I'm very grateful for all your labors.

Amber

Company: Anchor Hocking
Pattern: Block Optic
Color: Amber
Size: 1¾"
Value: $30.00

Company: Cambridge
Pattern: Cleo #437
Color: Amber
Size: 9"
Value: $85.00

Company: Cambridge
Pattern: Wildflower #647 double, "Keyhole"
Color: Amber gold encrusted
Size: 6"
Value: $125.00

Company: Duncan & Miller
Pattern: Caribbean #112, 3-ftd.
Color: Amber
Size: 2"
Value: $75.00

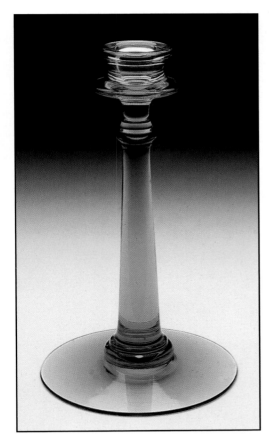

Company: Fostoria
Pattern: #2324
Color: Amber
Size: 9½"
Value: $40.00

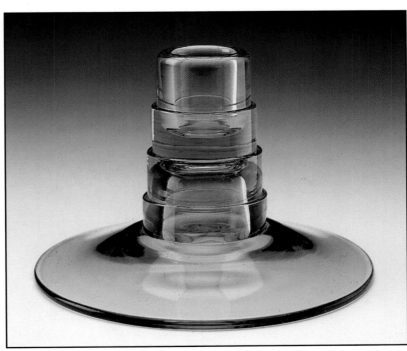

Company: Fostoria
Pattern: #2390
Color: Amber
Size: 3"
Value: $25.00

Company: Fostoria
Pattern: Baroque #2496, trindle
(Sakier design)
Color: Amber
Size: 5½" x 8¼"
Value: $75.00

Company: Fostoria
Pattern: Royal #2324
Color: Amber
Size: 4"
Value: $25.00

Company: Heisey
Pattern: Old Williamsburg #300, (tall base) double
Color: Amber (flashed)
Size: 16"
Value: $475.00

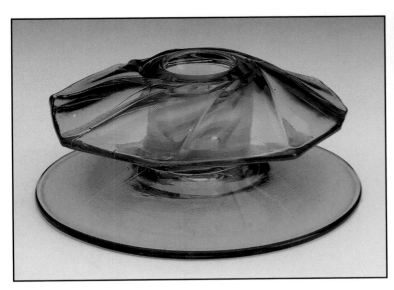

Company: Heisey
Pattern: Twist #1252
Color: Amber (Marigold)
Size: 2"
Value: $85.00

Company: L.E. Smith
Pattern: Romanesque #133
Color: Amber
Size: 2⁵⁄₁₆"
Value: $20.00

Company: Liberty Works
Pattern: American Pioneer
Color: Amber
Size: 6½"
Value: $75.00

Company: Paden City
Pattern: Black Forest Line #210, #531
Color: Amber
Size: 2½"
Value: $50.00

Company: Westmoreland
Pattern: #1049 Dolphin
Color: Amber
Size: 9"
Value: $65.00

Company: Westmoreland
Pattern: Lotus #1921
Color: Amber
Size: 3"
Value: $20.00

Company: Westmoreland
Pattern: Lotus #1921
Color: Amber
Size: 3⅞"
Value: $30.00

Black

Company: Cambridge
Pattern: #646 "Keyhole"
Color: Black (Ebony satinized)
Size: 5"
Value: $55.00

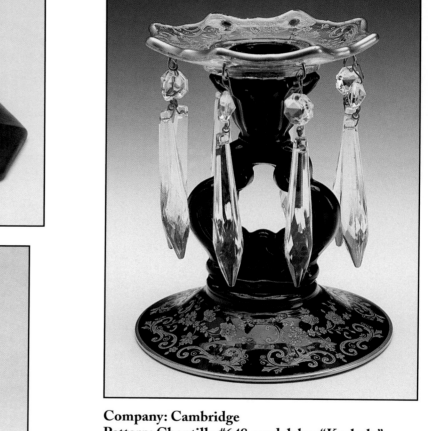

Company: Cambridge
Pattern: Chantilly #648 candelabra "Keyhole"
Color: Black (Ebony) w/gold
Size: 5"
Value: $125.00

Company: Cambridge
Pattern: Gloria #646 "Keyhole"
Color: Black (Ebony) w/white gold
Size: 6"
Value: $175.00

Company: Cambridge
Pattern: Square #3797/493
Color: Black (Ebony)
Size: 2¼"
Value: $25.00

Company: Cambridge
Pattern: Wildflower #648 candelabra "Keyhole"
Color: Black (Ebony) w/gold
Size: 6"
Value: $275.00

Company: Fenton
Pattern: Lincoln Inn
Color: Black
Size: 3⅞"
Value: $275.00

Company: Fostoria
Pattern: #2443 (Sakier design)
Color: Black (Ebony)
Size: 3½"
Value: $35.00

Company: Fostoria
Pattern: #2402
Color: Black (Ebony)
Size: 1½"
Value: $35.00

Company: Fostoria
Pattern: #2447 "even" duo (Sakier design)
Color: Black (Ebony)
Size: 5⅛" x 6½"
Value: $45.00

Company: Fostoria
Pattern: Cupid etch #288, #2324
Color: Black (Ebony)
Size: 4"
Value: $125.00

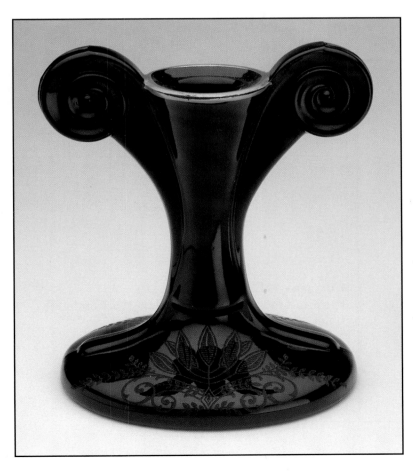

Company: Fostoria
Pattern: Fern #2395½ "Scroll"
Color: Black (Ebony) w/gold
Size: 5"
Value: $45.00

Company: Indiana
Pattern: Diamond Point
Color: Black
Size: 3¼"
Value: $12.50

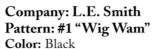
Company: L.E. Smith
Pattern: #1 "Wig Wam"
Color: Black
Size: 2¾"
Value: $30.00

Company: L.E. Smith
Pattern: #1402 (Greensburg Glass Works mould)
Color: Black
Size: 3"
Value: $25.00

Company: L.E. Smith
Pattern: Mt. Pleasant
"Double Shield"
(1933 World's Fair)
Color: Black
Size: 4½" x 5¾"
Value: $50.00

Company: L.E. Smith
Pattern: Mt. Pleasant "Double Shield" #600/4, double
Color: Black
Size: 4½" x 5¾"
Value: $25.00

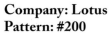

Company: Lotus
Pattern: #200
Color: Black w/gold Fleur de Lis
Size: 9"
Value: $55.00

Company: Paden City
Pattern: Regina #412, Ardith etch
Color: Black
Size: 4"
Value: $75.00

Company: Tiffin
Pattern: #315 "Twist"
Color: Black
Size: 9"
Value: $45.00

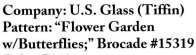

Company: U.S. Glass (Tiffin)
Pattern: "Flower Garden
w/Butterflies;" Brocade #15319
Color: Black
Size: 8"
Value: $175.00

Company: U.S. Glass (Tiffin)
Pattern: "Flower Garden w/Butterflies;"
Brocade #15319
Color: Black
Size: 6"
Value: $150.00; $250.00 w/brocade glass candle

Company: Westmoreland
Pattern: Lotus #1921
Color: Black
Size: 4"
Value: $40.00

19

Blue

Company: Cambridge
Pattern: #3900 /72 Caprice "Arch"
Color: Blue (Moonlight)
Size: 6"
Value: $65.00

Company: Cambridge
Pattern: #647 double "Keyhole"
Color: Blue (Windsor)
Size: 6"
Value: $300.00

Company: Cambridge
Pattern: Caprice #1338 triple; #744
Apple Blossom etch
Color: Blue (Moonlight)
Size: 6"
Value: $200.00

Company: Cambridge
Pattern: Caprice #1358
triple
Color: Blue (Moonlight)
Size: 6½"
Value: $325.00

Company: Cambridge
Pattern: Caprice #1338 triple
Color: Blue (Alpine)
Size: 6"
Value: $125.00

Company: Cambridge
Pattern: Caprice #69 double
Color: Blue (Moonlight)
Size: 7½"
Value: $750.00

Company: Cambridge
Pattern: Cleo etch; #627
Color: Blue (Willow)
Size: 4"
Value: $55.00

Company: Cambridge
Pattern: Caprice #70
Color: Blue (Alpine)
Size: 7"
Value: $75.00

Company: Cambridge
Pattern: Cleo etch; #638, 3-lite "Keyhole"
Color: Blue (Willow)
Size: 6"
Value: $150.00

Company: Cambridge
Pattern: Sea Shell
Color: Blue (Windsor)
Size: 1⅞"
Value: $45.00

Company: Cambridge
Pattern: Statuesque #3011
Color: Blue (Windsor)
Size: 9"
Value: $595.00

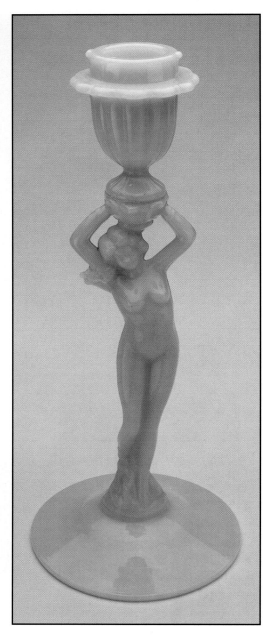

Company: Central Glass Works
Pattern: Morgan etch #412 (Balda design)
Color: Blue
Size: 3"
Value: $125.00

Company: Dalzell-Viking
Pattern: Janice #4554 REPRODUCTION
Color: Blue (cobalt)
Size: 5"
Value: $17.00

Company: Dalzell/Viking
Pattern: Candlewick 400/81 REPRODUCTION
Color: Blue w/blue satin
Size: 3¾"
Value: $15.00

Company: Dell
Pattern: Tulip
Color: Blue
Size: 3¾"
Value: $30.00

Company: Dell
Pattern: Tulip
Color: Blue
Size: 3⅜"
Value: $55.00

Company: Duncan & Miller
Pattern: Caribbean #112
Color: Blue
Size: 8"
Value: $195.00

Company: Fenton
Pattern: (Rambling) Rose (Tiffin mould)
Color: Blue (satinized)
Size: 10"
Value: $35.00

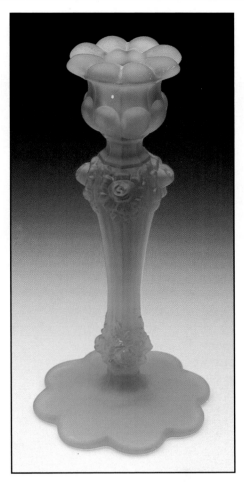

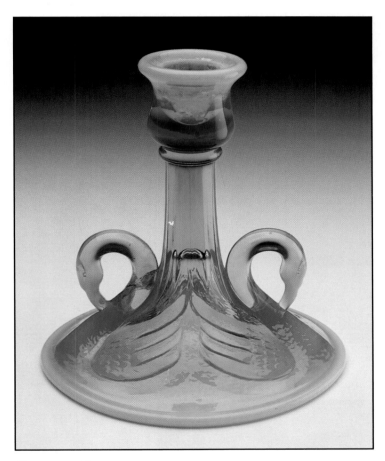

Company: Fenton
Pattern: Swan #6
Color: Blue Opalescent
Size: 5⅜"
Value: $200.00

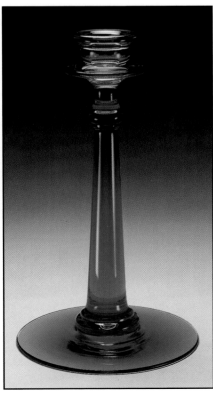

Company: Fostoria
Pattern: #2324
Color: Blue
Size: 8¾"
Value: $60.00

Company: Fostoria
Pattern: #2394
Color: Blue
Size: 2"
Value: $22.50

Company: Fostoria
Pattern: American #2056
Color: Blue
Size: 7¼"
Value: $350.00

Company: Fostoria
Pattern: Fairfax #2375½
Color: Blue (Azure)
Size: 2½"
Value: $25.00

Company: Fostoria
Pattern: #2545 "Flame" (Sakier design)
Color: Blue (Azure)
Size: 4½"
Value: $60.00

Company: Fostoria
Pattern: Kashmir etch #281, #2395½ "Scroll"
Color: Blue (Azure)
Size: 5"
Value: $42.50

Company: Fostoria
Pattern: Maypole #6149, #314
Color: Blue (Light)
Size: 3"
Value: $18.00

Company: Fostoria
Pattern: Meadow Rose etch #328,
Baroque #2496 (Sakier design)
Color: Blue (Azure)
Size: 5½"
Value: $75.00

Company: Fostoria
Pattern: Maypole #6149, #319
Color: Blue (Light)
Size: 9"
Value: $30.00

Company: Fostoria
Pattern: Quadrangle #2546
Color: Blue (Azure)
Size: 4¾" x 7¼"
Value: $125.00

Company: Fostoria
Pattern: Seascape #2685
Color: Blue Opalescent
Size: 2" x 4½"
Value: $35.00

Company: Fostoria
Pattern: Vesper etch #275, #2324
Color: Blue
Size: 4"
Value: $45.00

Company: H.C. Fry
Pattern: Unidentified
Color: Blue (Cornflower)
Size: 4½"
Value: $35.00

Company: Hazel Atlas
Pattern: Royal Lace (rolled)
Color: Blue (Ritz)
Size: 1⅞"
Value: $275.00

Company: Hazel Atlas
Pattern: Royal Lace (ruffled)
Color: Blue (Ritz)
Size: 2¼"
Value: $250.00

Company: Hazel Atlas
Pattern: Royal Lace (straight)
Color: Blue (Ritz)
Size: 2¼"
Value: $80.00

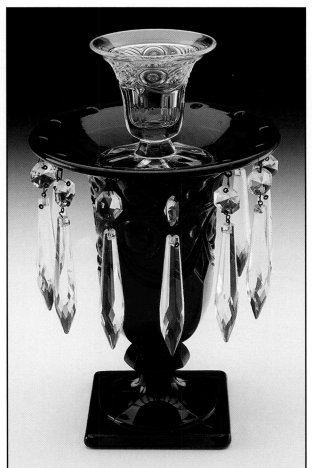

Company: Heisey
Pattern: Ipswich #1405 centerpiece, ftd., vase "A" prisms
Color: Blue (Cobalt)
Size: 9½"
Value: $750.00

Company: Heisey
Pattern: Old Williamsburg #301 (short base) double
Color: Blue (Cobalt)
Size: 10½"
Value: $1,500.00

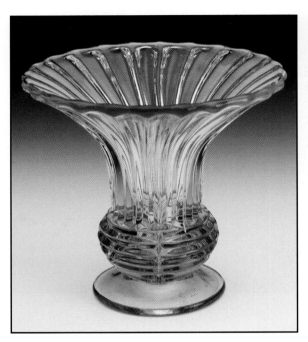

Company: Heisey
Pattern: Ridgeleigh #1469 originally candle vase
Color: Blue-Green (Zircon)
Size: 6"
Value: $115.00

Company: Heisey
Pattern: Saturn #1485 2-lite candelabrum
Color: Blue-Green (Zircon)
Size: 5"
Value: $500.00

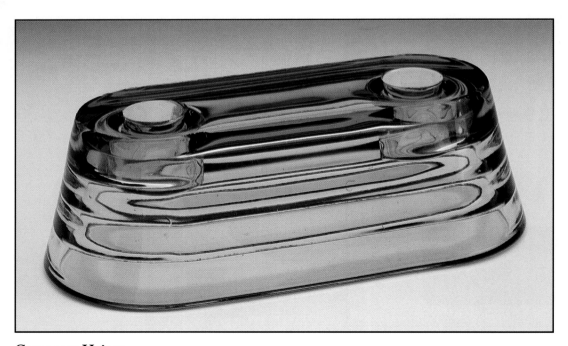

Company: Heisey
Pattern: Saturn #1485 2-lite candleblock
Color: Blue-Green (Zircon)
Size: 2"
Value: $350.00

Company: Imperial
Pattern: Diamond Quilted #414/1
Color: Blue
Size: 2¾"
Value: $25.00

Company: Imperial
Pattern: Laced Edge #7498
Color: Blue (Sea Foam)
Size: 4½"
Value: $30.00

Company: Imperial
Pattern: Reeded (Spun) #701
Color: Blue (Ritz)
Size: 2¾"
Value: $65.00

35

Company: Jeannette
Pattern: Adam
Color: Blue (Delphite)
Size: 4"
Value: $75.00

Company: Jeannette
Pattern: Swirl double
Color: Blue-green (Ultra Marine)
Size: 5½"
Value: $27.50

Company: L.E. Smith
Pattern: #1 "Wig Wam"
Color: Blue (Cobalt)
Size: 2¾"
Value: $35.00

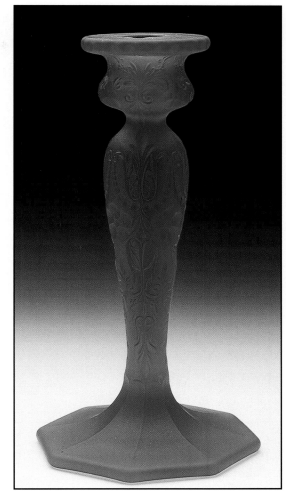

Company: McKee
Pattern: Early American Rock Crystal
Color: Blue (Jap)
Size: 8⅜"
Value: $95.00

Company: McKee
Pattern: Early American Rock Crystal double
Color: Blue (Ritz)
Size: 4½"
Value: $175.00

Company: Morgantown
Pattern: Golf Ball #7643 Jacobi
Color: Blue (Ritz)
Size: 4"
Value: $150.00

Company: New Martinsville
Pattern: Janice #4536 double
Color: Blue
Size: 5"
Value: $65.00

Company: New Martinsville
Pattern: Janice #4554
Color: Blue
Size: 5"
Value: $40.00

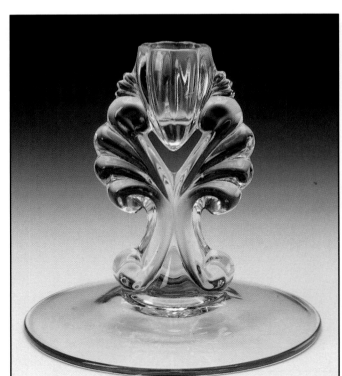

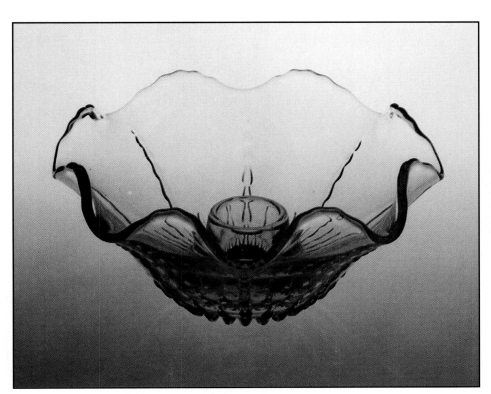

Company: New Martinsville
Pattern: Radiance #42, Line 4200, double
Color: Blue
Size: 6½"
Value: $95.00

Company: New Martinsville
Pattern: Radiance #42, ruffled
Color: Blue
Size: 3" x 6"
Value: $75.00

Company: New Martinsville
Pattern: Radiance #42, w/etch #26
("Meadow Wreath")
Color: Blue
Size: 6½"
Value: $95.00

Company: Paden City
Pattern: Crow's Foot #412
Color: Blue (Royal)
Size: 5⅜"
Value: $50.00

Company: Paden City
Pattern: Crow's Foot #412, Orchid etch
Color: Blue (Royal)
Size: 5⅜"
Value: $110.00

Company: Paden City
Pattern: Crow's Foot #412, silver overlay
Color: Blue (Royal)
Size: 5⅜"
Value: $70.00

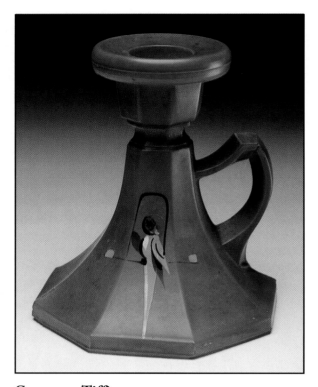

Company: Tiffin
Pattern: #17350
Color: Blue (Copen)
Size: 5"
Value: $50.00

Company: Tiffin
Pattern: Jungle Assortment #14 Parrot
Color: Blue (decorated)
Size: 4⅜"
Value: $35.00

Company: U.S. Glass (Tiffin)
Pattern: "Swirl"
Color: Blue
Size: 3⅜"
Value: $25.00

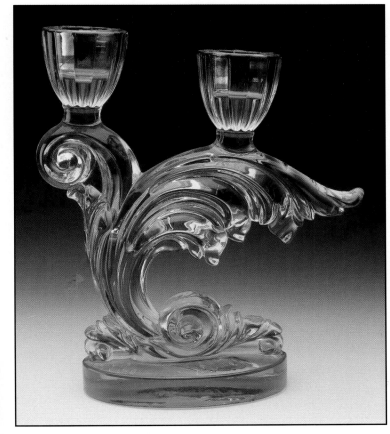

Company: Unidentified
Pattern: "Curling Wave" double
Color: Blue
Size: 8"
Value: $65.00

Company: Westmoreland
Pattern: English Hobnail #555
Color: Turquoise blue
Size: 8"
Value: $75.00

Company: Westmoreland
Pattern: Lotus #1921
Color: Blue (satinized)
Size: 3⁷⁄₈"
Value: $35.00

Company: Westmoreland
Pattern: Lotus #1921
Color: Blue (satinized)
Size: 4"
Value: $35.00

Crystal

Company: Anchor Hocking
Pattern: #981 "Stars & Bars"
Color: Crystal
Size: 1⁹⁄₁₆"
Value: $8.00

Company: Anchor Hocking
Pattern: Early American Prescut double
Color: Crystal
Size: 5¾"
Value: $32.00

Company: Anchor Hocking
Pattern: Manhattan
Color: Crystal
Size: ⅜" x 4½"
Value: $12.00

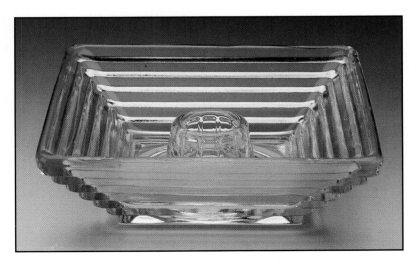

Company: Anchor Hocking
Pattern: Moonstone
Color: Crystal Opalescent
Size: 2½"
Value: $15.00

Company: Cambridge
Pattern: #1441 Epergne base
Color: Crystal
Size: 10⁵⁄₁₆"
Value: $100.00

Company: Cambridge
Pattern: #67 candle/"comport;"
#3900 Corinth
Color: Crystal
Size: 5"
Value: $25.00

Company: Cambridge
Pattern: Caprice #1577, 5-lite
Color: Crystal
Size: 4" x 9"
Value: $150.00

Company: Cambridge
Pattern: Caprice #67
Color: Crystal
Size: 2½"
Value: $15.00

Company: Cambridge
Pattern: Caprice #69 double
Color: Crystal
Size: 7½"
Value: $125.00

Company: Cambridge
Pattern: Elaine #3500/94 double
Color: Crystal
Size: 5¾"
Value: $75.00

Company: Cambridge
Pattern: Elaine #647, "Keyhole" double
Color: Crystal
Size: 6"
Value: $50.00

Company: Cambridge
Pattern: Everglade #1210
Color: Crystal w/cobalt epergne
Size: 9"
Value: $225.00 w/epergne; $50.00 w/o epergne

Company: Cambridge
Pattern: Farberware 2-lite
Color: Crystal
Size: 7½"
Value: $25.00

Company: Cambridge
Pattern: Ivy #1059
Color: Crystal
Size: 2½"
Value: $25.00

Company: Cambridge
Pattern: Heirloom #5000/70
Color: Crystal
Size: 9"
Value: $65.00

Company: Cambridge
Pattern: Moderne
Color: Crystal
Size: 2⅞"
Value: $25.00

Company: Cambridge
Pattern: Pristine #1616, 2-lite
Color: Crystal
Size: 6"
Value: $45.00

Company: Cambridge
Pattern: Rose Marie etch
#755, #1307 candelabrum
Color: Crystal
Size: 6⅛"
Value: $60.00

Company: Cambridge
Pattern: Rose Point #1613 hurricane
Color: Crystal
Size: 14"
Value: $395.00

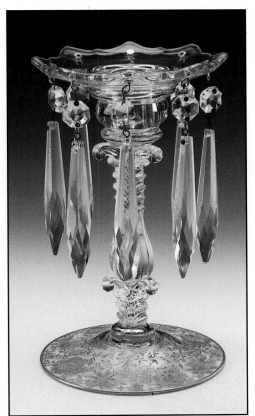

Company: Cambridge
Pattern: Rose Point #3121 candelabrum
Color: Crystal gold encrusted
Size: 7½"
Value: $225.00

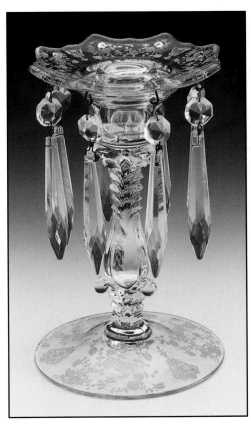

Company: Cambridge
Pattern: Rose Point #3121 candelabrum
Color: Crystal
Size: 7½"
Value: $175.00

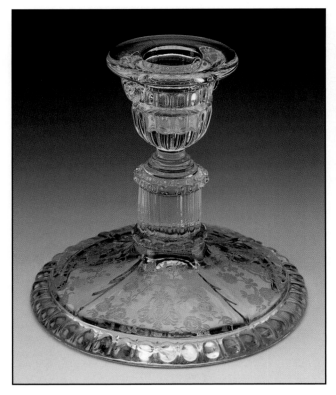

Company: Cambridge
Pattern: Rose Point #3500/74 "Ram's Head"
Color: Crystal
Size: 4"
Value: $75.00

Company: Cambridge
Pattern: Rose Point #3900/67
Color: Crystal
Size: 5"
Value: $70.00

Company: Cambridge
Pattern: Rose Point #500
Pristine (Leaf)
Color: Crystal
Size: 6½"
Value: $110.00

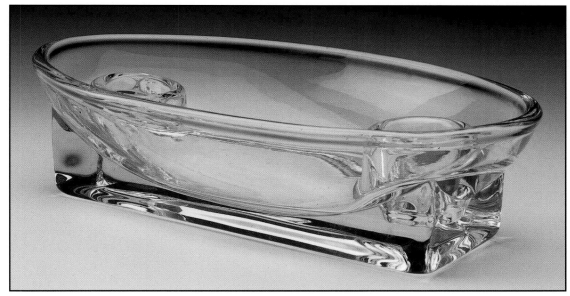

Company: Cambridge
Pattern: Square #3797
double
Color: Crystal
Size: 2" x 7½"
Value: $35.00

Company: Cambridge
Pattern: Square #3797/493
Color: Crystal
Size: 2¼"; 3¼"
Value: $20.00; 25.00

Company: Cambridge
Pattern: Square #3797/67
Color: Crystal
Size: 3"
Value: $15.00

Company: Cambridge
Pattern: Swan #1050
Color: Crystal
Size: 3" x 4½" w/candle insert
Value: $85.00

Company: Cambridge
Pattern: Wildflower #1268
2-lite candelabrum
Color: Crystal
Size: 6"
Value: $125.00

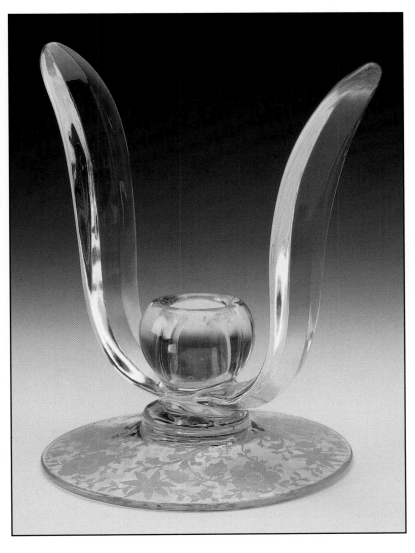

Company: Cambridge
Pattern: Wildflower #500 Pristine (Leaf)
Color: Crystal
Size: 6½"
Value: $90.00

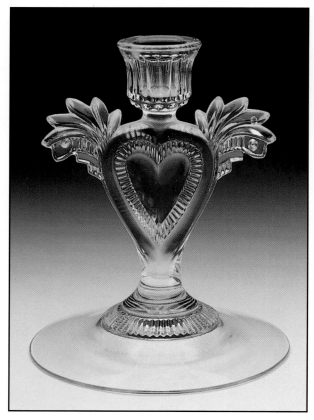

Company: Canton
Pattern: "Rib and Bead" #330
Color: Crystal
Size: 6⅜"
Value: $35.00

Company: Central Glass Works
Pattern: Harding #530
Color: Crystal
Size: 2¾"
Value: $45.00

Company: Colony
Pattern: Dogwood Blossom
Color: Crystal w/blue
Size: 1¼"
Value: $20.00

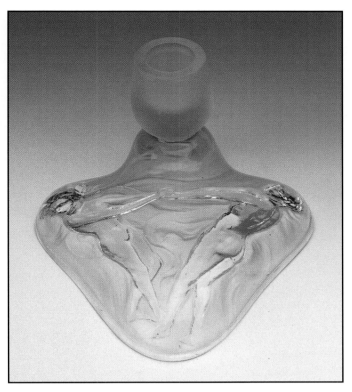

Company: Consolidated
Pattern: Dancing Nymphs
Color: Crystal (satinized)
Size: 3⅜"
Value: $200.00

Company: Consolidated
Pattern: Dancing Nymphs
Color: Crystal
Size: 3⅜"
Value: $175.00

Company: Duncan & Miller
Pattern: Canterbury #115, 3-lite, unidentified cut
Color: Crystal
Size: 6" x 10"
Value: $45.00

Company: Duncan & Miller
Pattern: First Love etch, Canterbury #115-121
Color: Crystal
Size: 3"
Value: $25.00

Company: Duncan & Miller
Pattern: Caribbean #112
Color: Crystal
Size: 5¼"
Value: $65.00

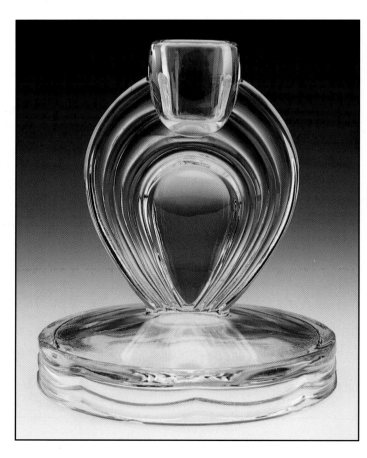

Company: Duncan & Miller
Pattern: "Grandee" candelabrum #14
Color: Crystal
Size: 8"
Value: $55.00

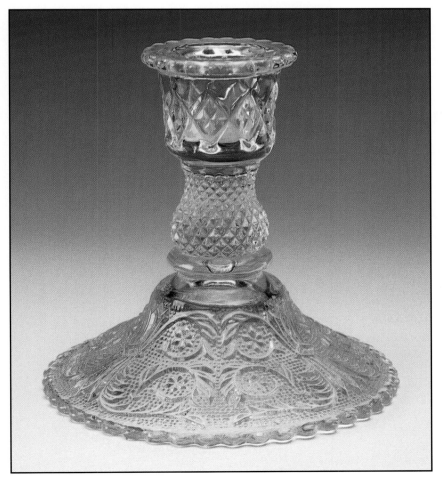

Company: Duncan & Miller
Pattern: Sandwich #41, #121
Color: Crystal
Size: 4¼"
Value: $25.00

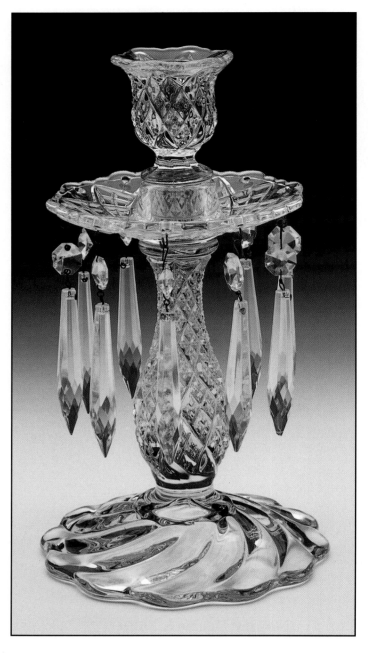

Company: Duncan & Miller
Pattern: Sandwich #41 w/bobeche & prisms
Color: Crystal
Size: 10"
Value: $85.00

Company: Fenton
Pattern: #449 oval cut
Color: Crystal
Size: 8½"
Value: $65.00

Company: Fenton
Pattern: #950 Cornucopia,
No. 43 Poinsettia decoration
Color: Crystal (satinized)
Size: 5¾"
Value: $25.00

Company: Fenton
Pattern: Silvertone #1010, 3-toed
Color: Crystal
Size: 1⅞"
Value: $15.00

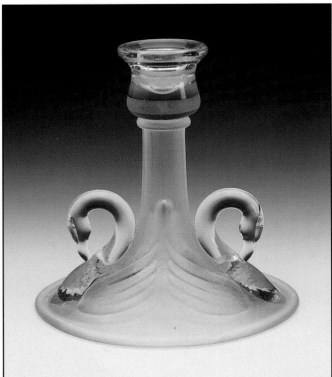

Company: Fenton
Pattern: Swan #6
Color: Crystal
Size: 5⅜"
Value: $65.00

Company: Fostoria
Pattern: #17 five-lite candelabra
Color: Crystal
Size: 23" x 15"
Value: $595.00

Company: Fostoria
Pattern: #2470½ unidentified cut
Color: Crystal
Size: 5½"
Value: $35.00

Company: Fostoria
Pattern: #2533 Duo "Leaf"
Color: Crystal
Size: 6¼"
Value: $35.00

Company: Fostoria
Pattern: #2535
Color: Crystal
Size: 5½"
Value: $35.00

Company: Fostoria
Pattern: #2636 "Plume" 2-lite
Color: Crystal
Size: 9½"
Value: $55.00

Company: Fostoria
Pattern: #2772/312 peg vase
Color: Crystal
Size: 7⅞"
Value: $20.00

Company: Fostoria
Pattern: #2772/334 trindle candle arm
Color: Crystal
Size: 2¼" x 7½"
Value: $25.00

Company: Fostoria
Pattern: #2772/460 candle/snack bowl
Color: Crystal
Size: 3" x 5"
Value: $15.00

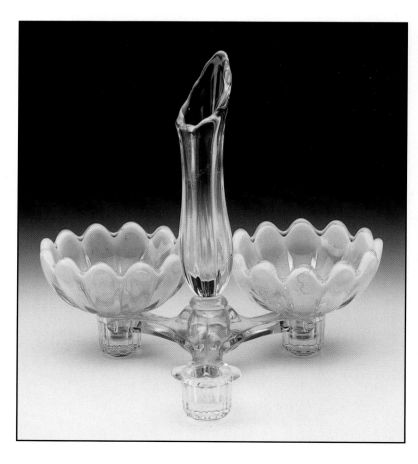

Company: Fostoria
Pattern: American #2056
Color: Crystal
Size: 7¼"
Value: $75.00

Company: Fostoria
Pattern: American #2056
candle lamp
Color: Crystal
Size: 8½"
Value: $135.00

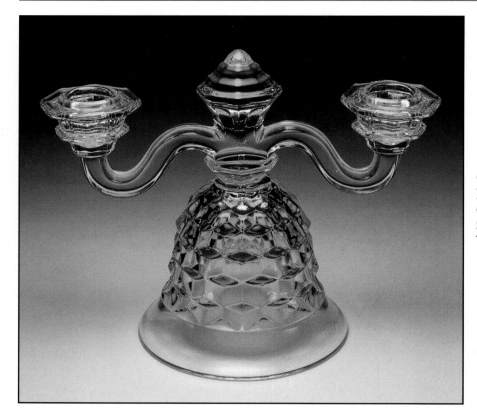

Company: Fostoria
Pattern: American #2056 Duo "Bell"
Color: Crystal
Size: 6½" x 8¼"
Value: $110.00

Company: Fostoria
Pattern: Baroque #2496 2-lite, 16 lustre
(Sakier design)
Color: Crystal
Size: 8¼" x 10"
Value: $95.00

Company: Fostoria
Pattern: Buttercup etch #340,
Baroque #2496 trindle (Sakier
design)
Color: Crystal
Size: 6" x 8¼"
Value: $60.00

Company: Fostoria
Pattern: Buttercup etch #340, #6023 "Step" duo
Color: Crystal
Size: 5⅜"
Value: $45.00

Company: Fostoria
Pattern: Century #2630
Color: Crystal
Size: 4½"
Value: $25.00

Company: Fostoria
Pattern: Century #2630 triple
Color: Crystal
Size: 7¾" x 7½"
Value: $40.00

Company: Fostoria
Pattern: Chintz etch #338, #6023
"Step" duo
Color: Crystal
Size: 5⅜"
Value: $95.00

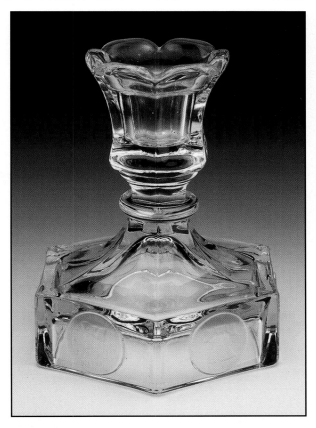

Company: Fostoria
Pattern: Coin #1372, #316
Color: Crystal
Size: 4½"
Value: $25.00

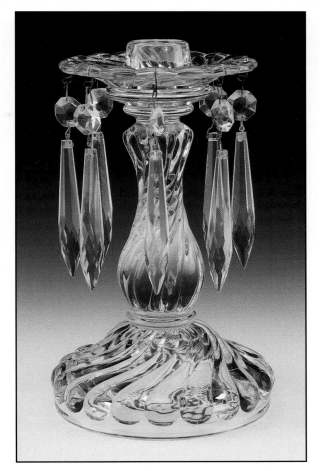

Company: Fostoria
Pattern: Colony #2412 w/8 "U" prisms
Color: Crystal
Size: 7½"
Value: $75.00

Company: Fostoria
Pattern: Coronet #2560, "Ram's Horn"
Color: Crystal
Size: 4½"
Value: $25.00

Company: Fostoria
Pattern: Corsage etch #325, #2545 "Flame" duo (Sakier design)
Color: Crystal
Size: 6¾" x 10¼"
Value: $65.00

Company: Fostoria
Pattern: Fuchsia etch #310, #2395½ "Scroll"
Color: Crystal
Size: 5"
Value: $40.00

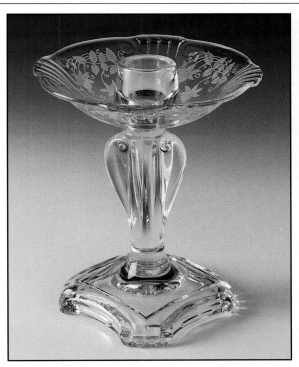

Company: Fostoria
Pattern: Fuchsia etch #310, #2470
Color: Crystal
Size: 5⅝"
Value: $55.00

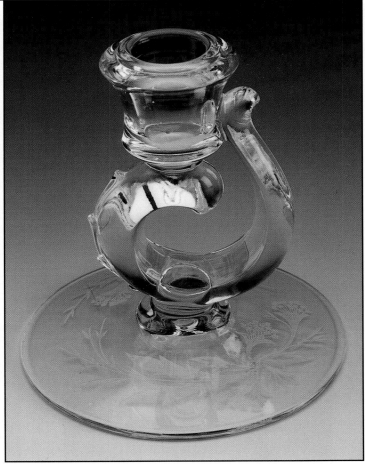

Company: Fostoria
Pattern: Heather etch #343, Century #2630
Color: Crystal
Size: 4½"
Value: $27.50

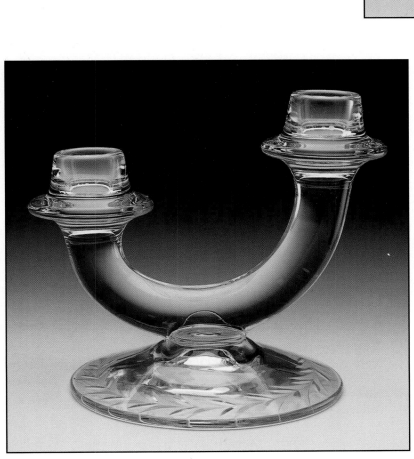

Company: Fostoria
Pattern: Holly cut #815,
#6023 "Step" duo
Color: Crystal
Size: 5½" x 6"
Value: $30.00

Company: Fostoria
Pattern: June etch #279, #2494
Color: Crystal
Size: 2"
Value: $25.00

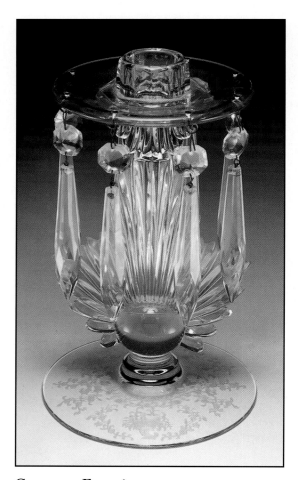

Company: Fostoria
Pattern: Mayflower etch #332, #2545 "Flame" (Sakier design)
Color: Crystal
Size: 6"
Value: $95.00

Company: Fostoria
Pattern: Mayflower etch #332, #2545 "Flame" (Sakier design)
Color: Crystal
Size: 4½"
Value: $40.00

Company: Fostoria
Pattern: Mayflower etch #332,
Coronet #2560 2-lite
Color: Crystal
Size: 4½"
Value: $50.00

Company: Fostoria
Pattern: Meadow Rose etch
#328, Sunray Line #2510,
2-lite (Sakier design)
Color: Crystal
Size: 6½" x 8"
Value: $175.00

Company: Fostoria
Pattern: Trindle Navarre etch
#327, Baroque #2496 (Sakier
design)
Color: Crystal
Size: 6" x 8¼"
Value: $65.00

Company: Fostoria
Pattern: Pine cut #835,
#2666 Contour
Color: Crystal
Size: 2" x 6"
Value: $20.00

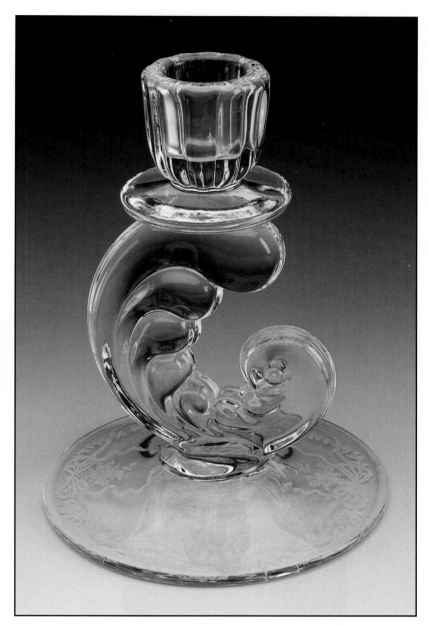

Company: Fostoria
Pattern: Romance etch #341, #2594
Color: Crystal
Size: 5⅝"
Value: $40.00

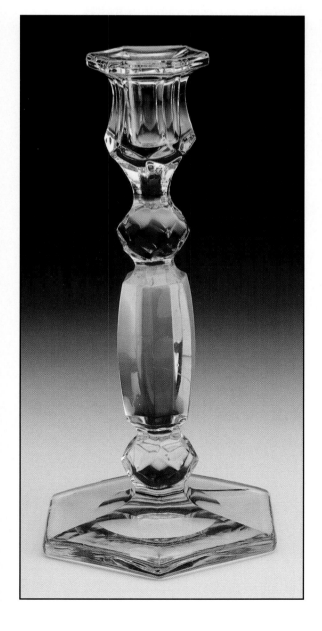

Company: Heisey
Pattern: #0001 Georgian
Color: Crystal
Size: 9"
Value: $85.00

Company: Heisey
Pattern: #5 Patrician
Color: Crystal
Size: 9"
Value: $65.00

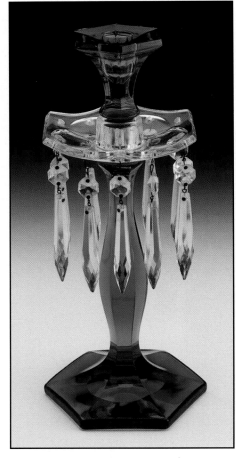

Company: Heisey
Pattern: #5 Patrician
Color: Crystal w/green (Moongleam)
Size: 12"
Value: $450.00

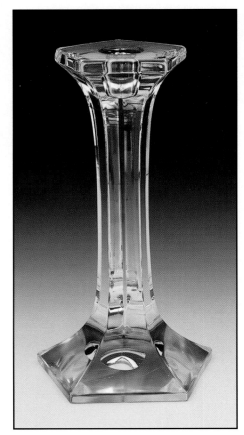

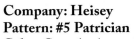

Company: Heisey
Pattern: #0016 Classic
Color: Crystal
Size: 9"
Value: $75.00

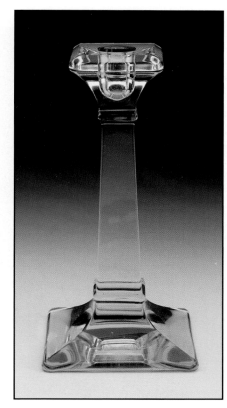

Company: Heisey
Pattern: #0021 Aristocrat
Color: Crystal
Size: 9"
Value: $75.00

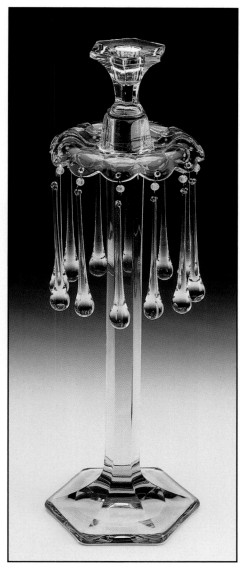

Company: Heisey
Pattern: #0018 Candelabrum
Color: Crystal
Size: 16"
Value: $325.00

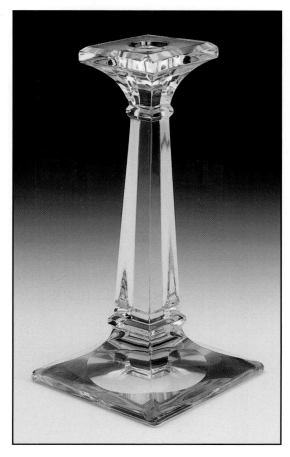

Company: Heisey
Pattern: #0021 Aristocrat
Color: Crystal
Size: 15"
Value: $75.00

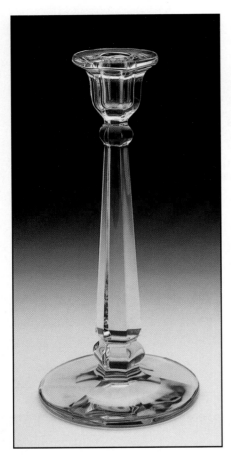

Company: Heisey
Pattern: #22 Windsor
Color: Crystal
Size: 11"
Value: $110.00

Company: Heisey
Pattern: #25 Federal
Color: Crystal
Size: 9"
Value: $45.00

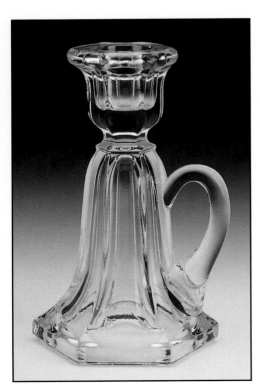

Company: Heisey
Pattern: #32 Skirted
Panel w/handle
Color: Crystal
Size: 7¼"
Value: $45.00

Company: Heisey
Pattern: #33 Skirted Panel
Color: Crystal
Size: 9"
Value: $75.00

Company: Heisey
Pattern: #99 "Little Squatter,"
candleblock
Color: Crystal
Size: 1¼"
Value: $15.00

Company: Heisey
Pattern: #116 Oak Leaf
Color: Crystal/Green (Moongleam)
Size: 3"
Value: $50.00

Company: Heisey
Pattern: #150 "Banded Flute," handled
Color: Crystal
Size: 2½"
Value: $40.00

Company: Heisey
Pattern: #300 Candle Lamp
Color: Crystal
Size: 18"
Value: $275.00

Company: Heisey
Pattern: #1445 "Grape Cluster" 2-lite
Color: Crystal
Size: 10"
Value: $125.00

Company: Heisey
Pattern: #1472 Parallel Quarter
Color: Crystal
Size: 3⁷⁄₁₆"
Value: $40.00

Crystal

Company: Heisey
Pattern: #1493 World
Color: Crystal
Size: 6"
Value: $300.00

Company: Heisey
Pattern: #1541 "Athena"
hurricane block
Color: Crystal
Size: 10"
Value: $140.00

Company: Heisey
Pattern: Crystolite #1503
Color: Crystal
Size: 4"
Value: $25.00

Company: Heisey
Pattern: Crystolite #1503 3-lite
Color: Crystal
Size: 4½"
Value: $45.00

Company: Heisey
Pattern: Formal Chintz
#134 Trident
Color: Crystal
Size: 5"
Value: $45.00

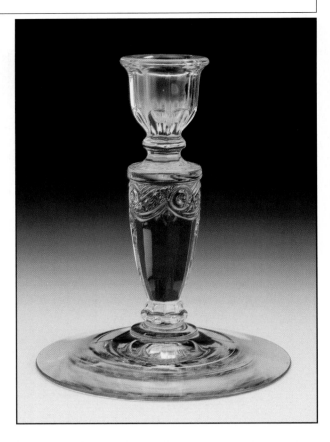

Company: Heisey
Pattern: Innovation #520
Color: Crystal w/unknown cut
Size: 4½"
Value: $100.00

Company: Heisey
Pattern: Ipswich #1405
Color: Crystal
Size: 6"
Value: $150.00

Company: Heisey
Pattern: Lariat #1540
(hurricane w/globe)
Color: Crystal
Size: 2¼" w/5" shade
Value: $95.00

Company: Heisey
Pattern: Leaf #1565
Color: Crystal
Size: 1½" x 6¾"
Value: $35.00

Company: Heisey
Pattern: Mercury #112,
Orchid etch #507
Color: Crystal
Size: 3"
Value: $40.00

Company: Heisey
Pattern: Minuet etch #1530;
Toujours #1511 centerpiece & vase
Color: Crystal
Size: 9½"
Value: $200.00

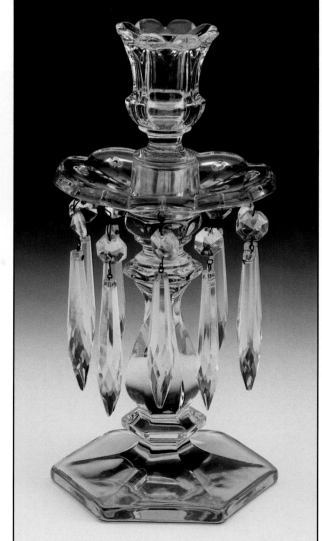

Company: Heisey
Pattern: Old Williamsburg #300-0 (tall base)
Color: Crystal
Size: 12"
Value: $95.00

Company: Heisey
Pattern: Old Williamsburg
#300-5 (tall base) 5-lite
Color: Crystal
Size: 25"
Value: $1,500.00

Company: Heisey
Pattern: Old Williamsburg #301
(short base) double
Color: Crystal
Size: 10½"
Value: $135.00

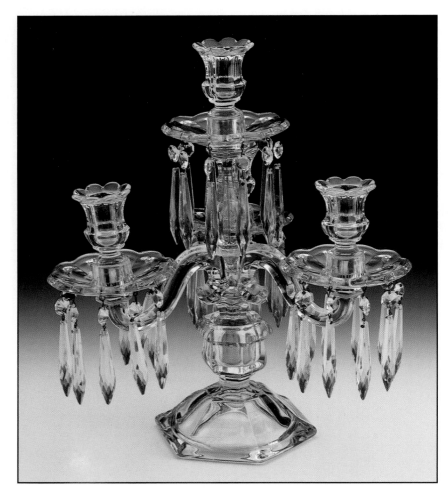

Company: Heisey
Pattern: Old Williamsburg
#301 (short base) 4-lite
Color: Crystal
Size: 14"
Value: $450.00

Company: Heisey
Pattern: Plantation #1567 3-lite
Color: Crystal
Size: 7"
Value: $140.00

Company: Heisey
Pattern: Plantation #1567, candleblock
Color: Crystal
Size: 3"
Value: $110.00

Company: Heisey
Pattern: Plantation #1567 epergne candle
Color: Crystal
Size: 5"
Value: $145.00

Company: Heisey
Pattern: Queen Anne #1509,
3-footed individual
Color: Crystal
Size: 1½" x 3"
Value: $50.00

Company: Heisey
Pattern: Ridgeleigh #1469
2-lite w/"A" prisms
Color: Crystal
Size: 11"
Value: $250.00

Company: Heisey
Pattern: Ridgeleigh #1469½, candelabra w/"A" prisms
Color: Crystal
Size: 10"
Value: $125.00

Company: Heisey
Pattern: Rose etch #1515, #112 Mercury
Color: Crystal
Size: 3⅝"
Value: $45.00

Company: Heisey
Pattern: Rose etch #1515, Waverly #1519 epergnette
Color: Crystal
Size: 3" x 6"
Value: $1,250.00

Company: Heisey
Pattern: Saturn #1485
2-lite candelabrum
Color: Crystal
Size: 5½" x 7½"
Value: $100.00

Company: Heisey
Pattern: Stanhope #1483, 2-lite
candelabra "A" prisms
Color: Crystal (satinized)
Size: 8"
Value: $195.00

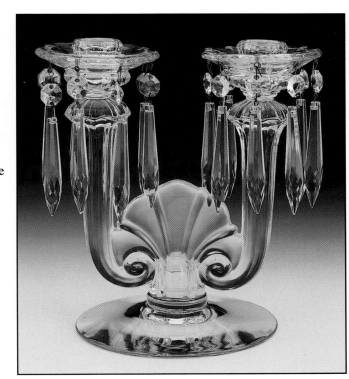

Company: Heisey
Pattern: Toujours #1511, 2-lite
bobeche & prisms
Color: Crystal
Size: 10"
Value: $140.00

Company: Heisey
Pattern: Warwick #1428 "Horn of Plenty"
Color: Crystal
Size: 2⁷⁄₁₆"
Value: $25.00

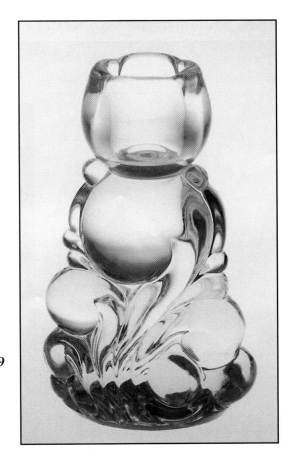

Company: Heisey
Pattern: Waverly #1519
Color: Crystal
Size: 4½"
Value: $65.00

Company: Heisey
Pattern: Waverly #1519 double
Color: Crystal w/cut
Size: 6½"
Value: $40.00

Company: Heisey
Pattern: Waverly #1519,
Orchid etch #507 3-lite
Color: Crystal
Size: 7½"
Value: $100.00

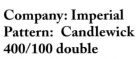

Company: Imperial
Pattern: Candlewick
400/100 double
Color: Crystal w/silver
orchid decorations
Size: 4¼"
Value: $60.00

Company: Imperial
Pattern: Candlewick 400/129R urn
Color: Crystal
Size: 6"
Value: $85.00

Company: Imperial
Pattern: Candlewick 400/207 3-toed
Color: Crystal
Size: 4½"
Value: $110.00

Company: Imperial
Pattern: Candlewick 400/224
Color: Crystal
Size: 5½"
Value: $175.00

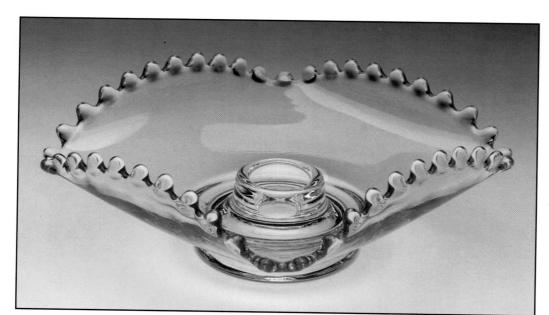

Company: Imperial
Pattern: Candlewick 400/40S
square
Color: Crystal
Size: 3" x 6"
Value: $65.00

Company: Imperial
Pattern: Candlewick 400/79 hurricane
Color: Crystal
Size: 10"
Value: $100.00

Company: Imperial
Pattern: Candlewick 400/79 hurricane
Color: Crystal w/red flashed flowers
Size: 10"
Value: $135.00

Company: Imperial
Pattern: Candlewick 400/79 hurricane
Color: Crystal w/red bird and floral decor
Size: 10"
Value: $150.00

Company: Imperial
Pattern: Candlewick 400/80
Color: Crystal
Size: 3½"
Value: $15.00

Company: Imperial
Pattern: Cape Cod #160/90 Aladdin style
Color: Crystal
Size: 4"
Value: $150.00

Company: Imperial
Pattern: "Crocheted Crystal," Laced Edge #78C
Color: Crystal
Size: 2"
Value: $20.00

Company: Imperial
Pattern: "Crocheted Crystal,"
Laced Edge #78K
Color: Crystal w/red flash
Size: 3"
Value: $40.00

Company: Imperial
Pattern: Old English
Color: Crystal
Size: 2⅜"
Value: $8.00

Company: Indiana
Pattern: Garland
Color: Crystal w/ stain
Size: 5½"
Value: $35.00

Company: Indiana
Pattern: King's Crown
Color: Crystal w/blue stain
Size: 3⅛"
Value: $25.00

Company: Indiana
Pattern: King's Crown
Color: Crystal w/red flash
Size: 3⅛"
Value: $25.00

Company: Indiana
Pattern: Sandwich #170
Color: Crystal
Size: 3½"
Value: $15.00

Company: Indiana
Pattern: "Teardrop"
Color: Crystal w/red flash
Size: 5½"
Value: $20.00

Company: Jeannette
Pattern: Anniversary
Color: Crystal
Size: 2½" x 4⅞"
Value: $10.00

Company: Jeannette
Pattern: Iris "Corsage" decoration styled by Century
Color: Crystal (satinized)
Size: 6¼"
Value: $30.00

Company: Jeannette
Pattern: National, 3-ftd.
Color: Crystal w/red flash
Size: 3"
Value: $18.00

Company: Jeannette
Pattern: "Pheasant"
Color: Crystal
Size: 2½" x 6⅜"
Value: $27.50

Company: Jeannette
Pattern: Windsor
Color: Crystal
Size: 3⅛"
Value: $12.50

Company: Jeannette
Pattern: Windsor, handled
Color: Crystal
Size: 1⅛"
Value: $18.00

Company: Lancaster
Pattern: Jubilee #833, cut #1200
Color: Crystal
Size: 2¾"
Value: $50.00

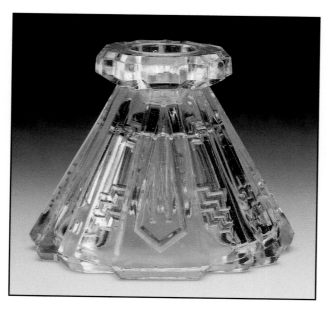

Company: L. E. Smith
Pattern: #1 "Wig Wam"
Color: Crystal
Size: 2¾"
Value: $15.00

Company: L. E. Smith
Pattern: #982, "Arrowhead" double
Color: Crystal
Size: 5¾"
Value: $17.50

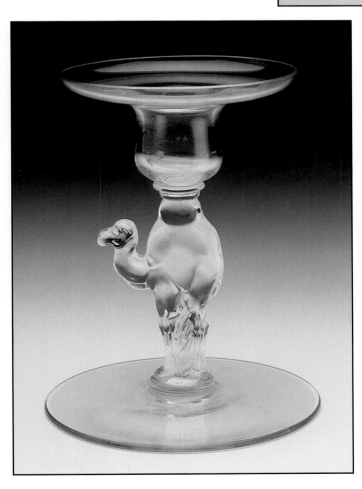

Company: Libbey
Pattern: Camel
Color: Crystal Opalescent
Size: 5"
Value: $150.00

Company: Lotus
Pattern: #201; La Furiste etch #0907
Color: Crystal w/gold
Size: 3½"
Value: $25.00

Company: McKee
Pattern: Early American
Rock Crystal
Color: Crystal
Size: 5½"
Value: $30.00

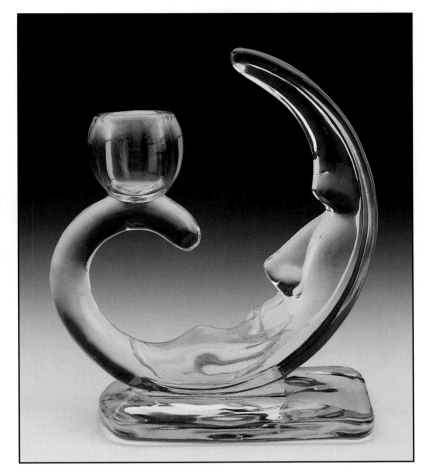

Company: New Martinsville
Pattern: "Man in Moon"
Color: Crystal
Size: 6¾"
Value: $100.00

Company: New Martinsville/ Viking
Pattern: #422-2V, 2-lite candelabrum
Color: Crystal
Size: 5½"
Value: $30.00

Company: Paden City
Pattern: Crow's Foot #890
Color: Crystal w/silver "Pine Cone" overlay
Size: 6"
Value: $35.00

Company: Paden City
Pattern: Crow's Foot #890
Color: Crystal
Size: 4"
Value: $35.00

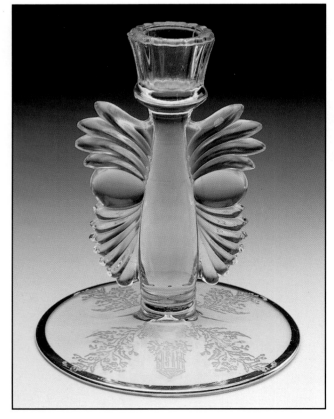

Company: Paden City
Pattern: Gazebo
Color: Crystal w/gold
Size: 6¼"
Value: $55.00

Company: Paden City
Pattern: Gazebo, #444 "Nine Ball" double
Color: Crystal
Size: 5"
Value: $55.00

Company: Paden City
Pattern: Gazebo, #555 double
Color: Crystal
Size: 5¾"
Value: $60.00

Company: Tiffin
Pattern: Flanders #15360 2-lite candelabrum
Color: Crystal
Size: 5⅛"
Value: $55.00

Company: Tiffin
**Pattern: Fuchsia hurricane,
Chinese style**
Color: Crystal
Size: 12"
Value: $275.00

Company: Tiffin
Pattern: King's Crown #4016, double
Color: Crystal w/red flash
Size: 6"
Value: $125.00

Company: Westmoreland
Pattern: Della Robia #1058 2-lite
Color: Crystal w/stain
Size: 6"
Value: $100.00

Company: Westmoreland
Pattern: Della Robia #1058
console set
Color: Crystal w/stain
Value: $350.00

Company: Westmoreland
Pattern: English Hobnail #555, 2-lite candelabra
Color: Crystal
Size: 6⅜"
Value: $20.00

Company: Westmoreland
Pattern: Lotus #1921
Color: Crystal
Size: 9"
Value: $45.00

Green

Company: Anchor Hocking
Pattern: Cameo
Color: Green
Size: 3¹¹⁄₁₆"
Value: $55.00

Company: Cambridge
Pattern: Caprice #1338 triple
Color: Green (Emerald dark)
Size: 6"
Value: $85.00

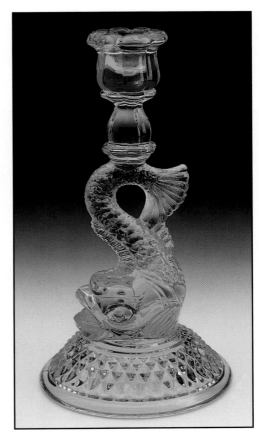

Company: Cambridge
Pattern: Dolphin candle #109
Color: Green (Emerald light)
Size: 9½"
Value: $150.00

Company: Cambridge
Pattern: Everglade #10
Color: Green (Emerald dark)
Size: 4"
Value: $30.00

Company: Cambridge
Pattern: Rosalie #731, #637
Color: Green (Emerald light)
Size: 3½"
Value: $40.00

Company: Consolidated
Pattern: Hummingbird & Orchid (no birds)
Color: Green (wash)
Size: 3⅛"
Value: $45.00

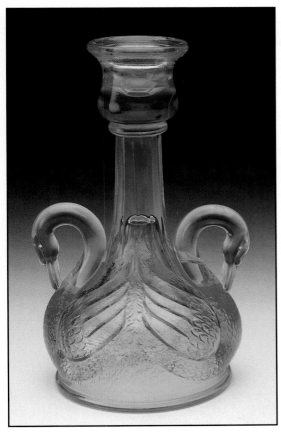

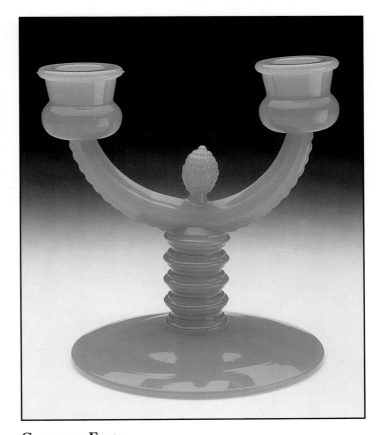

Company: Diamond
Pattern: Swan
Color: Green
Size: 6⅜"
Value: $55.00

Company: Fenton
Pattern: #2318 candelabra, double
Color: Green (Jade)
Size: 5¼"
Value: $65.00

Company: Fenton
Pattern: "Basket Weave" #1092
Color: Green Opal
Size: 2⅜" x 5"
Value: $25.00

Company: Fostoria
Pattern: Baroque #2496 (Sakier design)
Color: Green (Azure Tint)
Size: 4"
Value: $25.00

Company: Fostoria
Pattern: Baroque #2496 trindle (Sakier design)
Color: Green (Empire)
Size: 6"
Value: $125.00

Company: Fostoria
Pattern: Royal etch #273, #2324
Color: Green
Size: 2"
Value: $15.00

Company: Hazel Atlas
Pattern: Royal Lace (ruffled)
Color: Green
Size: 2¼"
Value: $65.00

Company: Heisey
Pattern: #116 Oak Leaf
Color: Green (Moongleam)/crystal
Size: 3"
Value: $50.00

Company: Heisey
Pattern: Ipswich #1405 centerpiece, ftd., vase "A" prisms
Color: Green (Moongleam)
Size: 9½"
Value: $450.00

Company: Heisey
Pattern: Warwick #1428 "Horn of Plenty"
Color: Green (Moongleam)
Size: 2⁷⁄₁₆"
Value: $135.00

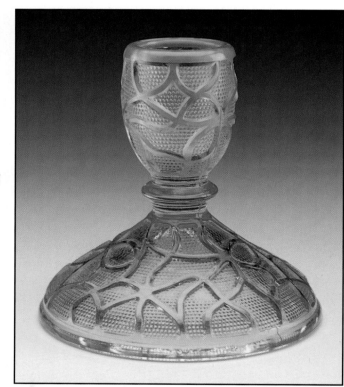

Company: Imperial
Pattern: "Tree of Life" #675
Color: Green
Size: 3¼"
Value: $20.00

Company: L.E. Smith
Pattern: #1 "Wig Wam"
Color: Green
Size: 2¾"
Value: $25.00

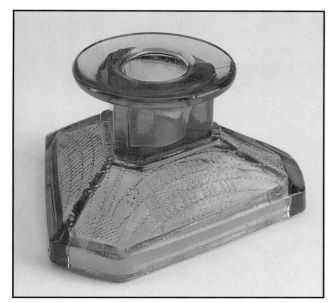

Company: L.E. Smith
Pattern: Romanesque #133
Color: Green
Size: 2⁵⁄₁₆"
Value: $22.00

Company: McKee
Pattern: Laurel, 3-footed
Color: Green (Jade)
Size: 1½"
Value: $65.00

Company: Paden Ciy
Pattern: #191 "Party Line"
Color: Green
Size: 4"
Value: $20.00

Company: Paden City
Pattern: "Peacock & Wild Rose" ("Nora Bird") #300
Color: Green
Size: 1¾" x 5"
Value: $70.00

Company: Tiffin
Pattern: Jungle Assortment #14 Parrot
Color: Green (decorated)
Size: 2¼"
Value: $30.00

Company: Tiffin
Pattern: Modern #6037
Color: Green (Kilarney)
Size: 4"
Value: $55.00

Company: Tiffin
Pattern: Swan
Color: Green (Kilarney)
Size: 4¾" x 6"
Value: $50.00

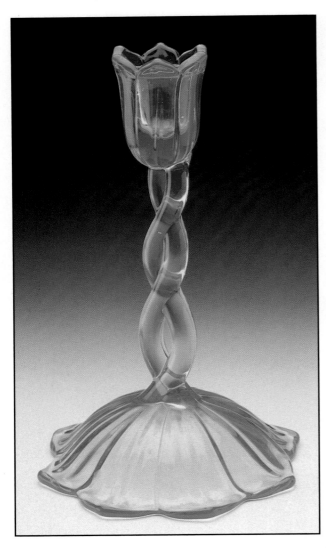

Company: Westmoreland
Pattern: Lotus #1921
Color: Green
Size: 9"
Value: $65.00

Company: Westmoreland
Pattern: Lotus #1921
Color: Green
Size: 3⅞"
Value: $35.00

Iridescent

Company: Imperial
Pattern: Candlewick 1950/170 (IGCS 1978)
Color: Iridescent Blue Carnival
Size: 1½"
Value: $40.00

Company: Jeannette
Pattern: Floragold
Color: Iridescent
Size: 5¼"
Value: $27.50

Company: Jeannette
Pattern: Anniversary
Color: Iridescent Carnival
Size: 2½" x 4⅞"
Value: $12.50

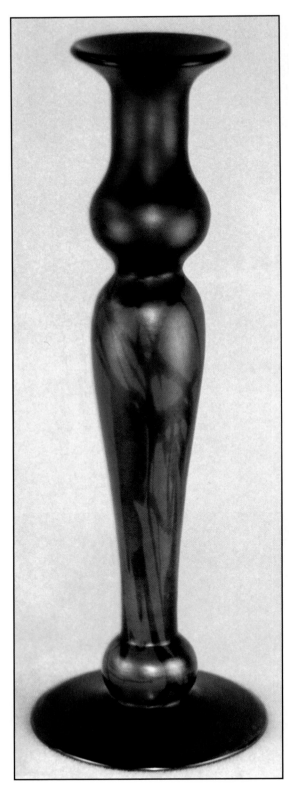

Company: Fenton
Pattern: Karnak Hanging Vine #3018
Color: Multi-color
Size: 11¾"
Value: $1,500.00

Company: Fenton
Pattern: Mosaic, #3027 one handled
Color: Multi-color
Size: 4¾"
Value: $600.00

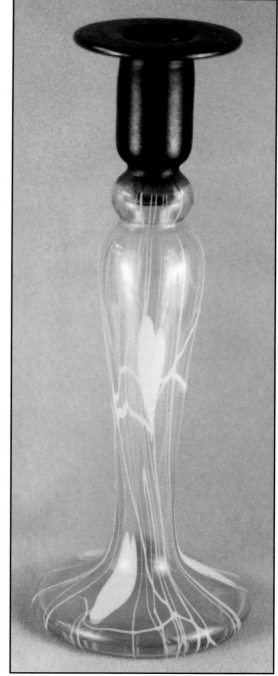

Company: Imperial
Pattern: Hanging Heart
Color: Multi-color
Size: 9⅞"
Value: $550.00

Company: Indiana
Pattern: #603
Color: Multi-color Orange/Beige
Size: 4"
Value: $15.00

Pink

Company: Anchor Hocking
Pattern: Old Colony
Color: Pink (Satinized)
Size: 3⅛"
Value: $35.00

Company: Cambridge
Pattern: Apple Blossom etch 3400/646 "Keyhole"
Color: Pink (Peach-Blo)
Size: 5¾"
Value: $55.00

Company: Cambridge
Pattern: Caprice #1338 triple
Color: Pink (La Rosa) (w/crosshatch)
Size: 6"
Value: $150.00

Company: Cambridge
Pattern: Cleo etch, #627
Color: Pink (Peach-Blo)
Size: 4"
Value: $45.00

Company: Cambridge
Pattern: Cleo etch, #638,
"Keyhole" 3-lite
Color: Pink (Peach-Blo)
Size: 6"
Value: $95.00

Company: Cambridge
Pattern: Cleo etch, #747
Color: Pink (Peach-Blo)
Size: 3"
Value: $75.00

Company: Cambridge
Pattern: Rosalie #731, #628
Color: Pink (Peach-Blo)
Size: 3½"
Value: $40.00

Company: Cambridge
Pattern: Valencia etch, #3500/31
Color: Pink (Peach-Blo)
Size: 6"
Value: $100.00

Company: Central Glass Works
Pattern: Harding #530
Color: Pink
Size: 2¹³⁄₁₆"
Value: $75.00

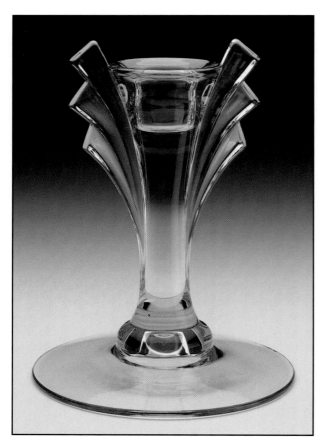

Company: Duncan & Miller
Pattern: #16
Color: Pink
Size: 6"
Value: $35.00

Company: Diamond
Pattern: "Flounce"
Color: Pink
Size: 3¼"
Value: $22.00

Company: Fostoria
Pattern: #2772/312 peg vase
Color: Crystal or pink
Size: 7⅞"
Value: $15.00 crystal; $35.00 pink

Company: Fostoria
Pattern: #2772/334 trindle candle arm
Color: Crystal
Size: 2¼" x 7½"
Value: $20.00

Company: Fostoria
Pattern: #2772/460 candle/snack bowl
Color: Crystal or pink
Size: 3" x 5"
Value: $15.00 crystal; $25.00 pink

Company: Fostoria
Pattern: Brocade, Palm Leaf, #2395½
Color: Pink Iridescent
Size: 5"
Value: $45.00

Company: Fostoria
Pattern: Century #2630
Color: Pink
Size: 4½"
Value: $100.00

Company: Fostoria
Pattern: Seascape #2685
Color: Pink Opalescent
Size: 2" x 4½"
Value: $35.00

Company: Fostoria
Pattern: Versailles etch #278, #2375
"Hex Collar"
Color: Pink (Rose)
Size: 3"
Value: $35.00

Company: H.C. Fry
Pattern: "Diamond Optic"
Color: Pink
Size: 3½"
Value: $30.00

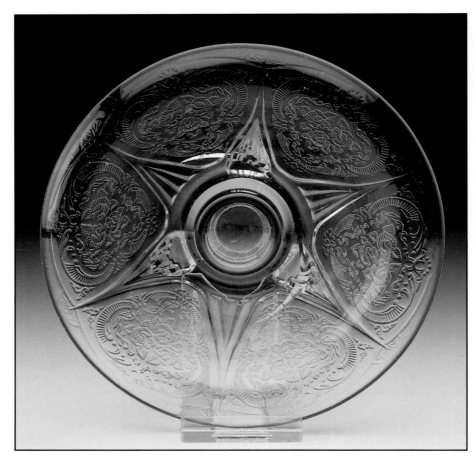

Company: Hazel Atlas
Pattern: Royal Lace (rolled)
Color: Pink
Size: 1⅞"
Value: $60.00

Company: Heisey
Pattern: "Miss Muffet" #118
Color: Pink (Flamingo)
Size: 3"
Value: $45.00

Company: Heisey
Pattern: "Little Squatter"
#99 candleblock
Color: Pink (Flamingo)
Size: 1¼"
Value: $25.00

Company: Heisey
Pattern: Pluto #114 , "Bubble Girl" etch
Color: Pink (Flamingo)
Size: 3½"
Value: $55.00

Company: Heisey
Pattern: Pluto #114 w/floral cut
Color: Pink (Flamingo)
Size: 3½"
Value: $35.00

Company: Jeannette
Pattern: #287 double
Color: Pink (Shell Pink)
Size: 5" x 6"
Value: $22.50

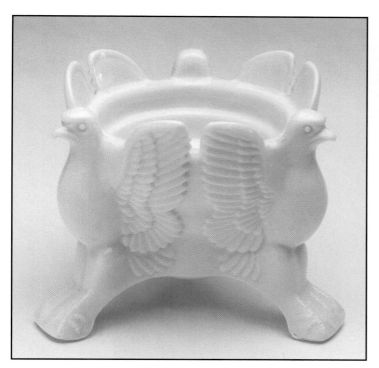

Company: Jeannette
Pattern: #3423
Color: Pink (Shell Pink)
Size: 3"
Value: $42.50

Company: Jeannette
Pattern: Floral
Color: Pink
Size: 4"
Value: $25.00

Company: Jeannette
Pattern: "Pheasant"
Color: Pink (Shell Pink)
Size: 2½" x 6⅜"
Value: $250.00

Company: Jeannette
Pattern: Windsor
Color: Pink
Size: 3¹⁄₁₆"
Value: $45.00

Company: Paden City
Pattern: "Crow's Foot"
Line #890, 3-lite
Color: Pink (Cheriglo)
Size: 6¼"
Value: $75.00

Company: New Martinsville
Pattern: "Moondrops", #37
Georgian Line
Color: Pink
Size: 1½"
Value: $35.00

Company: Westmoreland
Pattern: Lotus #1921
Color: Pink Opalescent
Size: 3⅞"
Value: $35.00

Company: Fostoria
Pattern: #2433 (Sakier design)
Color: Purple (Wisteria)
Size: 2¹⁵⁄₁₆"
Value: $90.00

Company: Fostoria
Pattern: #2447 "even" duo (Sakier design)
Color: Purple (Wisteria)
Size: 5⅛" x 6½"
Value: $75.00

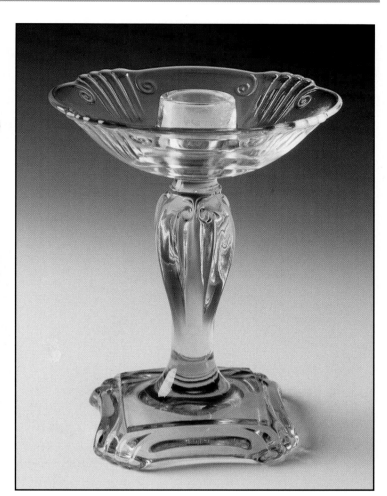

Company: Fostoria
Pattern: #2470
Color: Purple (Wisteria)
Size: 5⅝"
Value: $85.00

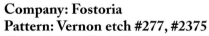

Company: Fostoria
Pattern: Vernon etch #277, #2375
Color: Purple (Orchid)
Size: 3"
Value: $25.00

Company: Heisey
Pattern: Mercury #112, cut unknown
Color: Purple (Hawthorne)
Size: 3"
Value: $50.00

Company: Heisey
Pattern: Pluto #114
Color: Purple (Hawthorne)
Size: 3½"
Value: $45.00

Company: Tiffin
Pattern: Garden set, #153-121, insert #153/198
Color: Purple (Twilight)
Size: 3" x 6"
Value: $125.00

Company: Anchor Hocking
Pattern: Oyster & Pearl #A881
Color: Red (Royal Ruby)
Size: 3¼"
Value: $30.00

Company: Cambridge
Pattern: Caprice #1338 triple
Color: Red (Carmen)
Size: 6"
Value: $250.00

Company: Cambridge
Pattern: Everglade #1211 3-pc. flower holder
Color: Red (Carmen)
Size: 9½"
Value: $1,000.00

Company: Cambridge
Pattern: Everglade #1211 candelabra
Color: Red (Carmen)
Size: 4" x 6"
Value: $400.00

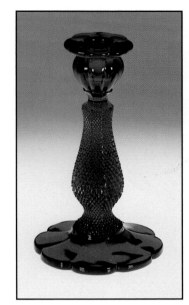

Company: Cambridge
Pattern: Mount Vernon #35
Color: Red (Carmen)
Size: 8"
Value: $125.00

Company: Cambridge
Pattern: Mount Vernon #38 candelabrum
Color: Red (Carmen)
Size: 13½"
Value: $300.00

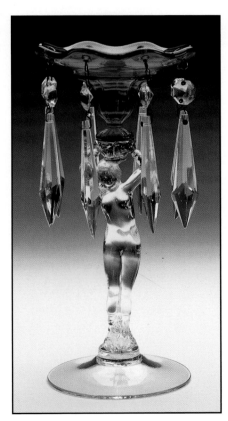

Company: Cambridge
Pattern: Statuesque #3011
Color: Red (Carmen)
Size: 9"
Value: $400.00

Company: Duncan & Miller
Pattern: Terrace #111
Color: Red
Size: 4"
Value: $40.00

Company: Fostoria
Pattern: Coin #1372, #326
Color: Red (Ruby)
Size: 8"
Value: $60.00

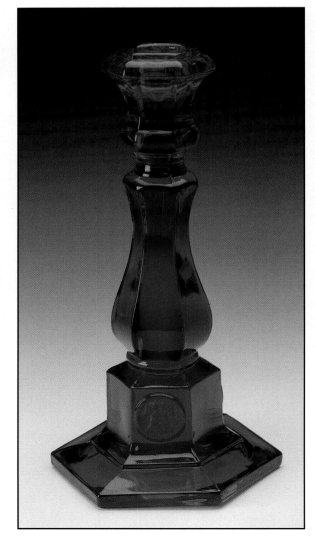

Company: Fostoria
Pattern: Heirloom #2726/311
Color: Red (Ruby)
Size: 3¹⁄₁₆"
Value: $27.00

Company: Imperial
Pattern: Candlewick 400/40C
Color: Red (Ruby)
Size: 3" x 6"
Value: $300.00

Company: Imperial
Pattern: "Hearts" #75
Color: Red (Ruby)
Size: 6⁹⁄₁₆"
Value: $75.00

Company: L.E. Smith
Pattern: Moon & Star
Color: Red
Size: 4½"
Value: $15.00

Company: L.G. Wright
Pattern: Moon and Star
Color: Amberina
Size: 6⅛"
Value: $20.00

Company: McKee
Pattern: Rock Crystal
Color: Red (Slag)
Size: 2¾"
Value: $125.00

Company: McKee
Pattern: Rock Crystal, 3-lite
Color: Red (Ruby)
Size: 6" x 6¾"
Value: $175.00

Company: New Martinsville
Pattern: Janice #4554
Color: Red (Ruby)
Size: 5¼"
Value: $45.00

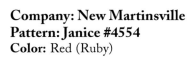

Company: New Martinsville
Pattern: "Moondrops," #37 Georgian Line
Color: Red (Ruby)
Size: 6"
Value: $125.00

Company: New Martinsville
Pattern: Radiance #42, ball
Color: Red (Ruby)
Size: 3"
Value: $65.00

Company: New Martinsville
Pattern: Radiance #42, candelabrum
Color: Red (Ruby)
Size: 8"
Value: $150.00

Company: Paden City
Pattern: Gadroon Line 881
Color: Red (Ruby)
Size: 6"
Value: $50.00

Company: Paden City
Pattern: Largo Line 220
Color: Red (Ruby)
Size: 5"
Value: $65.00

Company: Paden City
Pattern: Line #555, 2-lite
Color: Red (Ruby)
Size: 4½" x 6"
Value: $55.00

Company: Paden City
Pattern: "Crow's Foot" Line #890, 3-lite
Color: Red (Ruby)
Size: 6¼"
Value: $95.00

Company: Paden City
Pattern: Orchid etch, Line
#412; Crow's Foot
Color: Red (Ruby)
Size: 5"
Value: $100.00

Company: Paden City
Pattern: Penny Line #991
Color: Red (Ruby)
Size: 5¼"
Value: $25.00

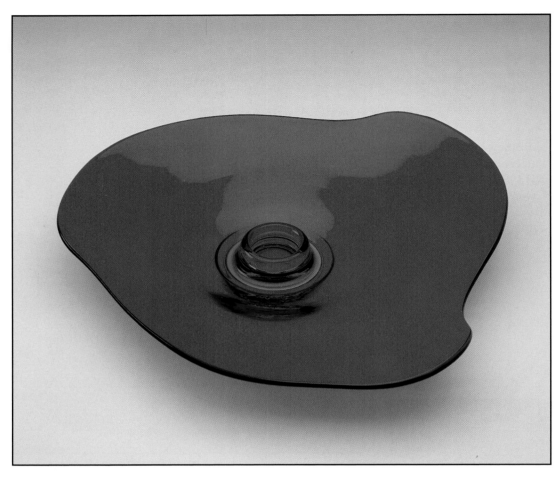

Company: Viking
Pattern: Epic #1100 Line Triangle
Color: Red (Orange)
Size: 1⅜" x 8⅝"
Value: $17.50

Company: Westmoreland
Pattern: Lotus #1921
Color: Amberina (Flame)
Size: 3"
Value: $25.00

Smoke

Company: Heisey
Pattern: Lodestar #1632;
Block #1543
Color: Smoke (Dawn)
Size: 2¾"
Value: $140.00

Company: Heisey
Pattern: Lodestar #1632
Color: Smoke (Dawn)
Size: 2"
Value: $65.00

White

Company: Duncan & Miller
Pattern: #120C, 3-lite candelabrum w/cut prisms
Color: White
Size: 11½"
Value: $800.00

Company: Imperial
Pattern: Grape 1950/137 double
Color: White
Size: 3½"
Value: $45.00

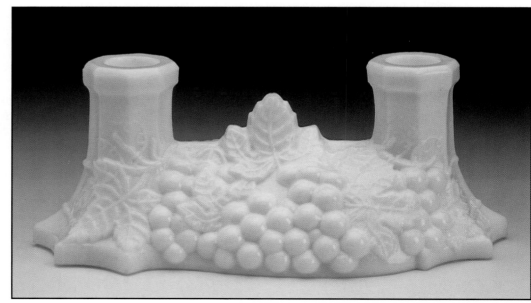

158

Company: Indiana
Pattern: "Wild Rose & Leaves"
Color: White
Size: 3"
Value: $6.00

Company: L.E. Smith
Pattern: Vintage Grape #9921
Color: White
Size: 2⅜" x 5"
Value: $15.00

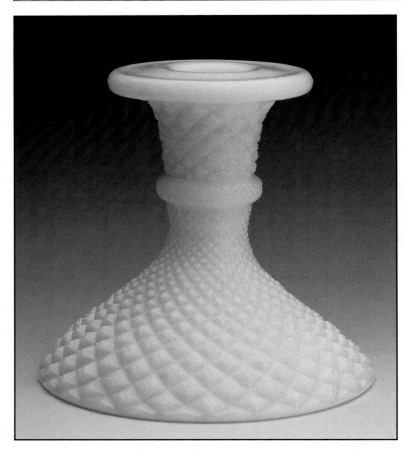

Company: Westmoreland
Pattern: English Hobnail #555, #71
Color: White
Size: 3⅜"
Value: $20.00

Company: Westmoreland
Pattern: Lotus #1921
Color: White
Size: 3⅞"
Value: $20.00

Company: Westmoreland
Pattern: Paneled Grape #1881,
3-lite candelabra
Color: White
Size: 4"
Value: $275.00

Company: Westmoreland
Pattern: Paneled Grape #1881,
colonial handled
Color: White
Size: 2¼" x 5⅛"
Value: $17.50

Yellow

Company: Cambridge
Pattern: #704
Color: Yellow
Size: 1½"
Value: $20.00

Company: Cambridge
Pattern: Apple Blossom etch #744; #626
Color: Yellow (Gold Krystol)
Size: 3⅞"
Value: $45.00

Company: Fostoria
Pattern: Line #2425
Color: Yellow, crystal
Size: 2½"
Value: $30.00

Company: Fostoria
Pattern: #2472 duo
Color: Yellow (Topaz)
Size: 4⅞" x 8"
Value: $35.00

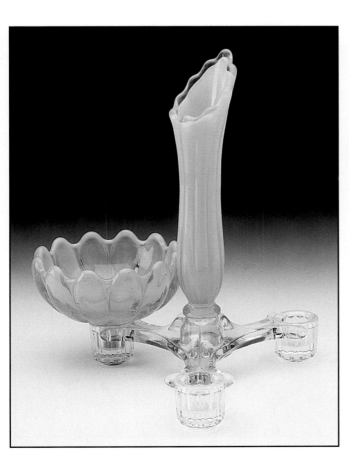

Company: Fostoria
Pattern: #2772/312 peg vase
Color: Yellow
Size: 7⅞"
Value: $35.00

Company: Fostoria
**Pattern: #2772/460 candle/
snack bowl**
Color: Yellow
Size: 3" x 5"
Value: $25.00

Company: Fostoria
Pattern: Fairfax, "Hex Collar" #2375
Color: Yellow (Topaz)
Size: 3"
Value: $20.00

Company: Fostoria
Pattern: Kashmir etch #283,
"Scroll" #2395½
Color: Yellow (Topaz)
Size: 5⅟₁₆"
Value: $35.00

Company: Fostoria
Pattern: Luxembourg Crown #2766, trindle candle bowl
Color: Yellow (Gold)
Size: 4½"
Value: $75.00

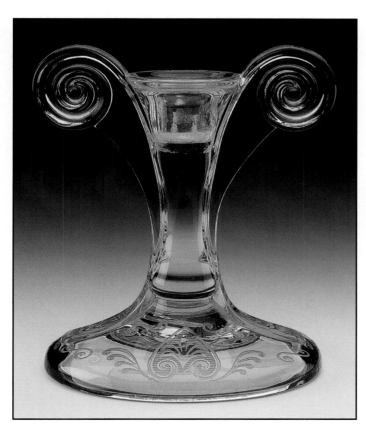

Company: Fostoria
Pattern: Trojan etch #280, "Scroll" #2395½
Color: Yellow (Topaz)
Size: 5¹⁄₁₆"
Value: $40.00

Company: Fostoria
Pattern: Versailles etch
#278, #2375½ Fairfax
Color: Yellow (Topaz)
Size: 2¾"
Value: $25.00

Company: Hazel Atlas
Pattern: Florentine #2
Color: Yellow
Size: 2¾"
Value: $35.00

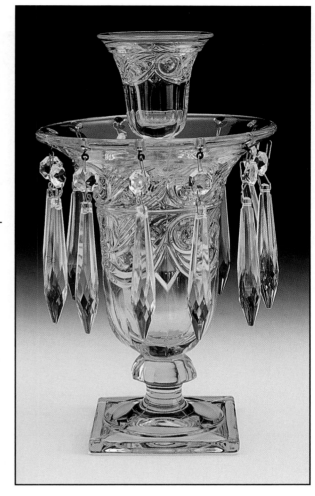

Company: Heisey
Pattern: Ipswich #1405 center-piece, ftd., vase "A" prisms
Color: Yellow (Sahara)
Size: 9½"
Value: $425.00

Company: Imperial
Pattern: Twisted Optic
Color: Yellow (Canary)
Size: 3⅜"
Value: $25.00

Company: Imperial
Pattern: Twisted Optic #637
Color: Yellow (Canary)
Size: 3¼"
Value: $25.00

Company: L.E.Smith
Pattern: Crackled #110
Color: Yellow (Canary)
Size: 2"
Value: $20.00

Company: Lancaster
Pattern: Jubilee   cut
#1200, #833 blank
Color: Yellow (Topaz)
Size: 2¾"
Value: $90.00

Company: Lancaster
Pattern: "Patrick" decoration #203,
#833 blank
Color: Yellow (Topaz)
Size: 2¾"
Value: $75.00

Company: Tiffin
Pattern: La Fleure #5831
Color: Yellow
Size: 3¾"
Value: $45.00

Company: Westmoreland
Pattern: Lotus #1921
Color: Yellow (cased)
Size: 3"
Value: $50.00

Index

Bibliography

Adt, Barbara. "Somewhere in Time ... George Sakier Designer, Fostoria Glass Company." *The Daze,* Feb. 1986.

Archer, Margaret and Douglas. *Imperial Glass.* Paducah, KY: Collector Books, 1978.

Barnett, Jerry. *Paden City, the Color Company.* Astoria, IL: Stevens Publishing Company, 1978.

Bickenheuser, Fred. *Tiffin Glassmasters.* Grove City, OH: Glassmasters Publication, 1979.

____. *Tiffin Glassmasters II.* Grove City, OH: Glassmasters Publication, 1981.

____. *Tiffin Glassmasters, III.* Grove City, OH: Glassmasters Publication, 1985.

Bones, Frances. *The Book of Duncan Glass.* Des Moines, IA: Wallace-Homestead Co., 1973.

Bredehoft, Neila and Tom. *Hobbs, Brockunier & Co., Glass.* Paducah, KY: Collector Books, 1997.

____. *The Collector's Encyclopedia of Heisey Glass, 1925 – 1938.* Paducah, KY: Collector Books, 1993.

Breeze, George & Linda. *Mysteries of the Moon & Star.* Paducah, KY: Image Graphics, Inc.

Burns, Mary Louise. *Heisey's Glassware of Distinction.* Mesa, AZ: Triangle Books, 1974.

Canton Glass Company, Inc. *Glassware by Canton.* Marion, IN: Canton Glass Company, 1954.

Conder, Lyle, Ed. *Collector's Guide to Heisey's Glassware for Your Table.* Glass City, IN: L.W. Book Sales, 1984.

Duncan & Miller Glass Co. *Hand-Made Duncan, Catalogue No. 89 (Reprint).* Washington, PA: Duncan & Miller Co., copyright pending by Richard Harold and Robert Roach.

Duncan & Miller, Inc. *Hand-made Duncan, Catalogue No. 93.* Tiffin, OH: Duncan & Miller Division, U.S. Glass Company, Inc.

Felt, Tom & Bob O'Grady. *Heisey Candlesticks, Candelabra & Lamps,* Newark, OH: Heisey Collectors of American, Inc., 1984.

Florence, Gene. *Elegant Glassware of the Depression Era, 8th Ed.* Paducah, KY: Collector Books, 1999.

____. *Collector's Encyclopedia of Depression Glass, 14th Ed.* Paducah, KY: Collector Books, 2000.

____. *Stemware Identification, 1920s – 1960s.* Paducah, KY: Collector Books, 1997.

____. *Collectible Glassware of the 40s, 50s, and 60s, 5th Ed.* Paducah, KY: Collector Books, 2000.

____. *Anchor Hocking's Fire-King and More.* Paducah, KY: Collector Books, 1998

Gallagher, Jerry. *A Handbook of Old Morgantown Glass, Vol. 1.* Minneapolis, MN: Merit Printing, 1995.

H.C. Fry Glass Society. *The Collector's Encyclopedia of Fry Glassware.* Paducah, KY: Collector Books, 1990.

Heacock, William. *Opalescent Glass from A to Z.* Marietta, OH: Richardson Printing Corp. 1975.

Kerr, Ann. *Fostoria.* Paducah, KY: Collector Books, 1997 update.

Kerr, Ann. *Fostoria, Vol. II.* Paducah, KY: Collector Books, 1997.

King, W.L. *Duncan & Miller Glass, Sec. Ed.* Venetia, PA: Victoria House Museum.

Krause, Gail. *The Encyclopedia of Duncan Glass.* Hicksville, NY: Exposition Press, 1976.

McGrain, Patrick, Ed. *Fostoria, The Popular Years.* Frederick, MD: McGrain Publications, 1983.

Measell, James. *New Martinsville Glass, 1900 – 1944.* Marietta, OH: Antique Publications, 1994.

____. *Fenton Glass, The 1980s Decade.* Marietta, OH: Glass Press, Inc. 1996.

____, editor. *Imperial Glass Encyclopedia, Vol. I.* National Imperial Glass Collectors' Society. Marietta, OH: The Glass Press, Inc., 1995.

____, editor. *Imperial Glass Encyclopedia, Vol. II.* Marietta, OH: The Glass Press, Inc., 1997.

Miller, Everett R. and Addie R. *The New Martinsville Glass Story Book II, 1920 – 1950.* Manchester, MI, Rymack Printing Company, 1975.

Nat'l. Cambridge Collectors, Inc. *Genuine Handmade Cambridge, 1949 – 1953.* Paducah, KY: Collector Books, 1978.

____. *The Cambridge Glass Co., 1930 – 1934.* Paducah, KY: Collector Books, 1976.

____. *Colors in Cambridge Glass.* Paducah, KY: Collector Books, 1984.

Newark Heisey Collectors Club, *Heisey by Imperial and Imperial Glass by Lenox.* Newark, OH: Heisey Collectors of America, Inc. 1980.

Newbound, Betty and Bill. *Collector's Encyclopedia of Milk Glass.* Paducah, KY: Collector Books, 1998.

Page, Bob and Dale Frederiksen. *A Collection of American Crystal.* Greensboro, NC: Page-Frederiksen Publishing Company, 1995.

____. *Tiffin is Forever*. Greensboro, NC: Page-Frederiksen Publishing Co., 1994.

Ream, Louise, Neila M., and Thomas H. Bredehoft. *Encyclopedia of Heisey Glassware, Vol. 1*. Newark, OH: Heisey Collectors of America, Inc., 1977.

Sferrazza, Julie. *Farber Brothers, Krome Kraft*. Marietta, OH: Antique Publications, 1988.

Stout, Sandra McPhee. *The Complete Book of McKee*. N. Kansas City, KS: The Trojan Press, 1972.

____. *Depression Glass, Number One*. Des Moines, IA: Wallace-Homestead, 1970.

____. *Depression Glass, Number Two*. Des Moines, IA: Wallace-Homestead, 1971.

____. *Heisey on Parade*. Lombard, IL: Wallace-Homestead, 1985.

Viking Glass Company. *Treasured American Glass*. New Martinsville, WV: Viking Glass Company.

Vogel, Clarence W. *Heisey's First Ten Years...1896 – 1905*. Plymouth, OH: Heisey Publications, 1969.

____. *Heisey's Colonial Years...1906 – 1922*. Plymouth, OH: Heisey Publications, 1969.

____. *Heisey's Art and Colored Glass, 1922 – 1942*. Plymouth, OH: Heisey Publications, 1970.

____. *Heisey's Early and Late Years, 1896 – 1958*. Plymouth, OH: Heisey Publications, 1971.

Walker, Mary Lyle and Lynn. *The Cambridge Glass Co.* Newark, OH: Spencer Walker Press, 1974.

Weatherman, Hazel Marie. *Colored Glassware of the Depression Era 2*. Springfield, MO: Weatherman Glassbooks, 1974.

____. *Fostoria, Its First Fifty Years*. Springfield, MO: The Weathermans, 1979.

____. *Price Trends to Colored Glassware of the Depression Era, Book 2*. Springfield, MO: Weatherman Glass Books, 1979.

Whitmyer, Margaret & Kenn. *Fenton Art Glass, 1907 – 1939*. Paducah, KY: Collector Books, 1996.

Wilson, Charles West. *Westmoreland Glass*. Paducah, KY: Collector Books, 1996.

Wilson, Jack D. *Phoenix and Consolidated Art Glass: 1926 – 1980*. Marietta, OH: Antique Publications, 1996.